THE LORE OF
SPICES

THE LORE OF
SPICES

Their history, nature and uses around the world

J.O.SWAHN

SENATE PUBLISHING LTD
LONDON

This edition published by Senate Publishing LTD, Twickenham,
by arrangement with Nordbok International.

Printcd and bound in Portugal 1999

ISBN 1-84056-040-1

———————————————

THE LORE OF SPICES has been originated, designed and produced by
AB Nordbok, Gothenburg, Sweden.

Editorial chief: Ingela Bruce
Graphic design: Munir Lotia
Artwork: Ulf Söderqvist
Consultant: Ingvar Nordin
(Gothenburg Botanical Garden)
Translator: Jon van Leuven

Nordbok would like to express special thanks to
Andras Banovits (Gothenburg University Library) and
Ingrid Skoglund (Gothenburg Botanical Library)
for their contributions to this book.

Contents

Preface

*T*he idea of a new, all-round book about spices has long been entertained by both our versatile author, Jan-Öjvind Swahn, and the publishers. After several years of collaboration, this search for the secrets of superb tastes has proved to be even more enlightening and colourful than we expected. Here the cultural history of spices is woven together with as much botanical knowledge as useful advice and anecdotes about some of the most precious plants on our planet.

After its general introductory chapter, the book divides spices into four headings that reflect their geographical origins. The individual chapters on selected spices include a fact-block with information about the plant's accepted names (in scientific terms and five foreign languages), its spicy part, origin, and main countries of cultivation. We have chosen to mention only countries that both grow and export the spice in question; on the same basis, a map of spice production is shown (pages 8-9). The result is not an exhaustive picture of mankind's almost limitless use of spices, but a broad view of the conditions under which these wonderful, often weird organisms come into the world.

The relationships between spice families are clarified by an illustration (pages 202-203), according to the system of Professor Carl Skottsberg, a leading Swedish botanist. The beautiful, detailed colour plates — from volumes published in past centuries — were provided by the Botanical Library at Gothenburg University and the private collection of library counsellor Nils Sandberg.

We hope that readers will find the subject as appetizing, and discover as many fresh approaches to it, as all of us have done while producing THE LORE OF SPICES.

Spice countries around the world

Spices today are produced and exported mainly by the countries indicated here — not including the many places where spices are grown on a small scale for private use. Countries that cultivate individual spices are also listed in their respective chapters.

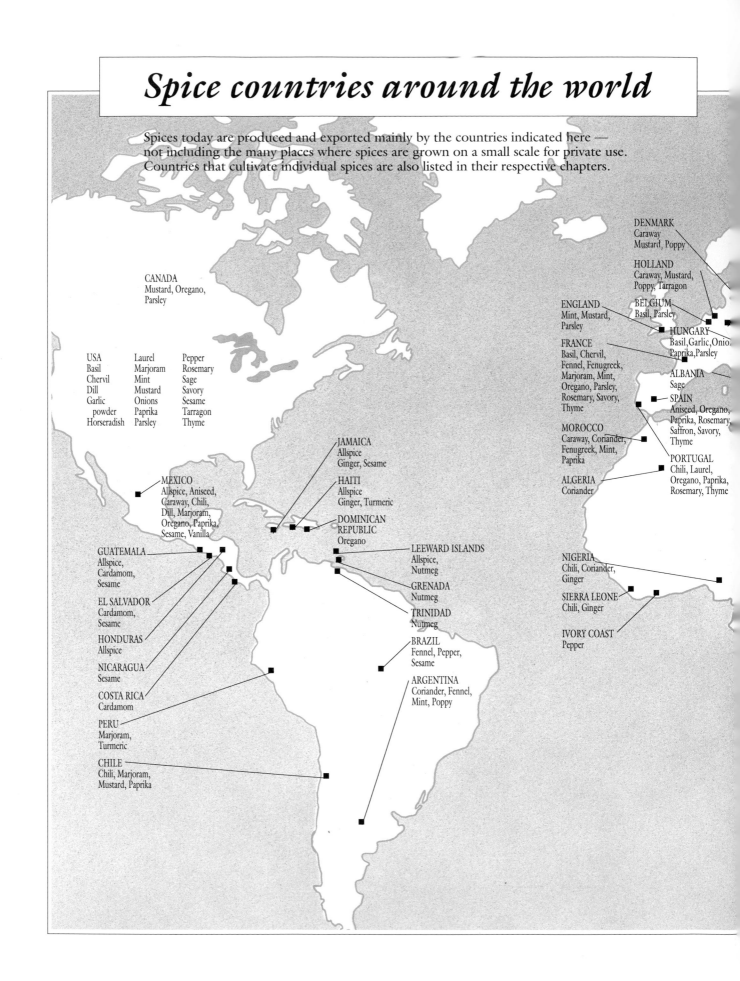

CANADA
Mustard, Oregano, Parsley

USA
Basil
Chervil
Dill
Garlic powder
Horseradish
Laurel
Marjoram
Mint
Mustard
Onions
Paprika
Parsley
Pepper
Rosemary
Sage
Savory
Sesame
Tarragon
Thyme

MEXICO
Allspice, Aniseed, Caraway, Chili, Dill, Marjoram, Oregano, Paprika, Sesame, Vanilla

GUATEMALA
Allspice, Cardamom, Sesame

EL SALVADOR
Cardamom, Sesame

HONDURAS
Allspice

NICARAGUA
Sesame

COSTA RICA
Cardamom

PERU
Marjoram, Turmeric

CHILE
Chili, Marjoram, Mustard, Paprika

JAMAICA
Allspice
Ginger, Sesame

HAITI
Allspice
Ginger, Turmeric

DOMINICAN REPUBLIC
Oregano

LEEWARD ISLANDS
Allspice, Nutmeg

GRENADA
Nutmeg

TRINIDAD
Nutmeg

BRAZIL
Fennel, Pepper, Sesame

ARGENTINA
Coriander, Fennel, Mint, Poppy

DENMARK
Caraway
Mustard, Poppy

HOLLAND
Caraway, Mustard, Poppy, Tarragon

ENGLAND
Mint, Mustard, Parsley

BELGIUM
Basil, Parsley

HUNGARY
Basil, Garlic, Onion, Paprika, Parsley

FRANCE
Basil, Chervil, Fennel, Fenugreek, Marjoram, Mint, Oregano, Parsley, Rosemary, Savory, Thyme

ALBANIA
Sage

SPAIN
Aniseed, Oregano, Paprika, Rosemary, Saffron, Savory, Thyme

MOROCCO
Caraway, Coriander, Fenugreek, Mint, Paprika

PORTUGAL
Chili, Laurel, Oregano, Paprika, Rosemary, Thyme

ALGERIA
Coriander

NIGERIA
Chili, Coriander, Ginger

SIERRA LEONE
Chili, Ginger

IVORY COAST
Pepper

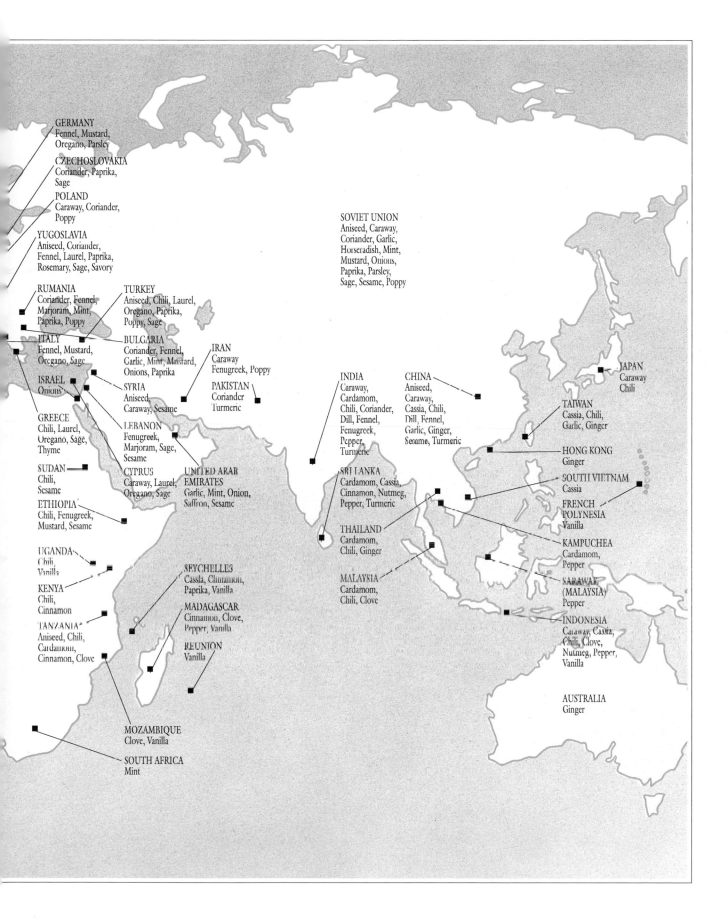

GERMANY
Fennel, Mustard,
Oregano, Parsley

CZECHOSLOVAKIA
Coriander, Paprika,
Sage

POLAND
Caraway, Coriander,
Poppy

YUGOSLAVIA
Aniseed, Coriander,
Fennel, Laurel, Paprika,
Rosemary, Sage, Savory

RUMANIA
Coriander, Fennel,
Marjoram, Mint,
Paprika, Poppy

ITALY
Fennel, Mustard,
Oregano, Sage

ISRAEL
Onions

GREECE
Chili, Laurel,
Oregano, Sage,
Thyme

SUDAN
Chili,
Sesame

ETHIOPIA
Chili, Fenugreek,
Mustard, Sesame

UGANDA
Chili,
Vanilla

KENYA
Chili,
Cinnamon

TANZANIA
Aniseed, Chili,
Cardamom,
Cinnamon, Clove

TURKEY
Aniseed, Chili, Laurel,
Oregano, Paprika,
Poppy, Sage

BULGARIA
Coriander, Fennel,
Garlic, Mint, Mustard,
Onions, Paprika

SYRIA
Aniseed,
Caraway, Sesame

LEBANON
Fenugreek,
Marjoram, Sage,
Sesame

CYPRUS
Caraway, Laurel,
Oregano, Sage

IRAN
Caraway
Fenugreek, Poppy

PAKISTAN
Coriander
Turmeric

UNITED ARAB
EMIRATES
Garlic, Mint, Onion,
Saffron, Sesame

SEYCHELLES
Cassia, Cinnamon,
Paprika, Vanilla

MADAGASCAR
Cinnamon, Clove,
Pepper, Vanilla

REUNION
Vanilla

MOZAMBIQUE
Clove, Vanilla

SOUTH AFRICA
Mint

SOVIET UNION
Aniseed, Caraway,
Coriander, Garlic,
Horseradish, Mint,
Mustard, Onions,
Paprika, Parsley,
Sage, Sesame, Poppy

INDIA
Caraway,
Cardamom,
Chili, Coriander,
Dill, Fennel,
Fenugreek,
Pepper,
Turmeric

SRI LANKA
Cardamom, Cassia,
Cinnamon, Nutmeg,
Pepper, Turmeric

THAILAND
Cardamom,
Chili, Ginger

MALAYSIA
Cardamom,
Chili, Clove

CHINA
Aniseed,
Caraway,
Cassia, Chili,
Dill, Fennel,
Garlic, Ginger,
Sesame, Turmeric

JAPAN
Caraway
Chili

TAIWAN
Cassia, Chili,
Garlic, Ginger

HONG KONG
Ginger

SOUTH VIETNAM
Cassia

FRENCH
POLYNESIA
Vanilla

KAMPUCHEA
Cardamom,
Pepper

SARAWAK
(MALAYSIA)
Pepper

INDONESIA
Caraway, Cassia,
Chili, Clove,
Nutmeg, Pepper,
Vanilla

AUSTRALIA
Ginger

Spices in a nutshell

Spices are by no means simply part of our daily existence. They belong to those festive moments in which we put the final touches to a culinary creation for breathless guests. Not a day goes by without our palates and pinkies coming in contact with all manner of spices that have streamed together in our kitchens from the far corners of the earth. Each and every one of them has its own background in nature, as well as in cultural history. And this book is intended to unite those two aspects with what is perhaps the most important, gastronomy.

What are spices, anyway?

The question may seem needless—who doesn't know that? But neither need it be debated. There is no argument that spices include pepper and cardamom. On the other hand, why mention Japanese soya, onions, tomato puré, or the salty mashed fillets in an anchovy soufflé? Indeed, where is the boundary between spices and preservatives? Salt and sugar have played both of these roles.

Spices also have much in common with drugs and medicines. Did people begin to use cloves in food because they were thought to taste good, or because—like ginger and cardamom—they had a reputation as aphrodisiacs? Moreover, some spices are used mainly in our drinks, such as hops in beer, juniper in gin and geneva, wormwood in vermouth: these should not be forgotten.

The spice trade has long been profitable for governments as well as merchants. This was the "Old Custom House" at London's East India Wharf, painted by Samuel Scott in 1756.

A spice dealer in Madras, southern India—one of the exotic places connected with aromatic spices.

The budding of taste

How long the human race has known the uses of spices, we cannot even estimate in numbers of millennia. But it is pretty certain that the spicing of foods in one way or another is a custom almost as ancient as the very craft of cooking. And cooking is about as old as the greatest of all discoveries, namely when prehistoric people learned to use fire. The taming of fire was what made it possible for humans—unlike other animal species—to prepare food instead of just eating it raw. This was perhaps the most important cultural revolution ever. Culture begins with cooking: boiled or fried meat could be eaten much more quickly than raw flesh, saving time for people to devote to other things than chewing, such as thought and creativity.

No known culture in history, or among the "primitive" folk of our age, has been totally ignorant of spices. We can safely assume that spices in general belong to the earliest features of human life—to the first companions of mankind.

Yet spices are ephemeral things, and archaeologists have not found much to contribute to their tale. Nevertheless, many prehistoric peoples had a tradition of caring for their departed relatives by providing for a comfortable existence beyond the grave. Thus, for example, their burials often included clay pots containing food for a journey to the afterworld. From dried traces of food and drink, on potsherds that date back thousands of years, it is clear that some Europeans in the Bronze Age—3,500 years ago—knew how to spice beer with the same bitter herbs which their descendants enjoy today. At the same time, spices in countries such as Greece were being celebrated by documents of international trade and remarkable works of art that still earn our fascination.

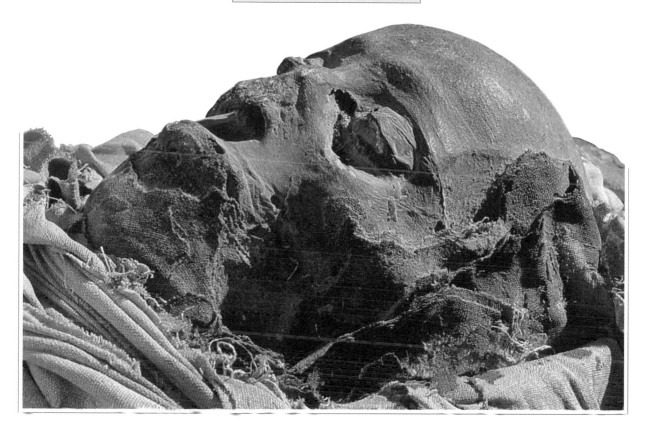

Ancient Egyptians used huge quantities of spices, not only for cooking but also to mummify the dead.

Even in ancient Egypt...

Spices first emerge in all their glory from the pages of history, though, in ancient Egypt. The people of the Pharaohs were great consumers of spices, not only in daily life but also afterward—as mummies. Indeed, a mummy was just an unusually well-spiced cadaver, pickled in pounds of cumin, anise, marjoram, cassia and other exotic substances.

The Egyptians were also familiar with using spices for far more purposes than we are accustomed to. Aristocrats burned cinnamon in their palaces so that its scent would hide the stench from the crowds outside.

In addition, Egyptian pharmacies were veritable warehouses of spices, as most spices were also thought to have pharmaceutical properties. Obviously this was a society which needed an organized spice trade in order to function. Even a couple of thousand years before Christ, huge quantities of spices were shipped westward from India, besides the already-mentioned cardamom and pep-

per. Thus began the spice trade between East and West, which was to have enormous effects on economic and political life as well as culture.

A monarchic meeting

Around 950 B.C., King Solomon of Israel had a sumptuous visitor in his capital, Jerusalem. The Queen of Sheba arrived at the head of a caravan, whose camels swayed under gifts of gold and spices. The Bible tells in detail how impressed she was by his palace and its wealth. Reading between the lines, however, one senses that she did not come primarily to pay her respects. In fact she wanted to "test him with hard questions". What these were is not stated, but they presumably had to do with trading policies.

Solomon, together with King Hiram of Tyre, had equipped a merchant fleet, based at Eilat on the Red Sea, with fine ships built of cedar from Lebanon. This maritime activity aimed, among other things, to obtain spices from nearer their sources—in the land of Ophir—so as to cut out the profits of entrepreneurs. Exactly where Ophir lay is a mystery, yet the candidates have included India, eastern Africa and Oman.

At any rate, the entrepreneur most likely to be threatened by this development was the Sheban kingdom (now Yemen) in southern Arabia. Its transit trade by caravan was the target of the Phoenician effort. So its queen had every reason to "question" Solomon about his future role in the shipping business.

The Israelites' oceanic adventure seems to have been short, and never reduced the Shebans' commercial status. What did, though, were the sailors who, at the time of Christ, found that regular voyages could be made in both easterly and westerly directions, according to the monsoon winds. These enabled spices to be sailed right past the Sheban realm, which thus fell into decline. Other Arab trade centres arose to deal with spices, and profited by supplying Eastern aromas to gourmets in the Roman Empire.

Extravagant appetites

Whoever wants to prepare food with the cookbook attributed to a Roman gourmet named Apicius must have a well-stocked spice cupboard. Around sixty kinds of spices were used regularly in his kitchen. Some of them are familiar to us, but others we should be almost glad to avoid. One of the Romans' favourite aromatics, named "garum", was similar to modern Worcester sauce, yet made from fermented fish intestines.

A surviving recipe for flamingo—whose tongue was considered the best part, on a level with kid tongue—called for garum as well as pepper, lovage, celery seeds, sesame, parsley, mint, onions, dates, wine and other ingredients. With so much seasoning, the taste and quality of the basic material were doubtless of minor importance.

Nearly a dozen of the spices that the Romans liked best were imported from far to the east, particularly the Malabar Coast of India. Brought up into the Red Sea by the monsoon sailors' ships, they were handed over to the wholesalers of Alexandria, who would long remain the hub in the spice trade's wheel of international distribution.

Other seasonings came by caravan from Persia and countries beyond—such as tibast, a most malodorous treat for the taste. These spices were shipped first to the Phoenician coastal ports in the Levant, such as Tyre. But they, too, eventually had to await export at Alexandria, whose only real competition arose at Constantinople.

The Romans, in turn, conducted their own transit trade in spices, which they sent to their provinces in France and England, as well as to the Germanic peoples of northern Europe. The latter were evidently fond of spices: when Alaric, king of the Visigoths, burned Rome in the year 410, more than two tons of pepper were on the list of booty desired by this scarcely fastidious general.

Darkness in the kitchen

Ancient food culture and its love of spices vanished during the medieval folk migrations from north and east. Refined Roman customs of cooking were forgotten, and the barbarians who took power had primitive ways of eating. The Huns from central Asia kept their beef under their horse-saddles, to be seasoned with the animals' sweat and tenderized by the beating rhythm of the ride. Germanic chieftains settled in the fields which had supported ancient civilization, and the nobility that replaced the old Roman patricians was peasant-like by comparison. Grilled steaks and boiled pork were bolted down, and washed down with beer or—where available —wine.

Predictably, the main spice to reach Europe during these Dark Ages was hop, a seasoning for beer which we still adore. For some centuries, Oriental spices were very expensive rarities in the West. It therefore aroused great attention when the king of France once donated more than half a kilogram of cinnamon to a monastery in Normandy.

In time, a new aristocracy sprouted from the rulers of these Germanic tribes, and more sophisticated customs developed. But in the new feudal Europe of the high Middle Ages, what decisively taught the rough barons and counts a modicum of manners—not least at the dinner table—were the Crusades in the eleventh and twelfth centuries.

What the Crusaders really won

The armies of knights who invaded the countries just east of the Mediterranean Sea got to know the culture of the Muslims, and above all of the Arabs, who were far more refined and educated than contemporary Europeans. Among all that the Frenchmen, Englishmen, Germans and Italians now experienced thanks to the Arabs, not the least were Oriental spices. The "holy wars" gave Europe a whetted appetite for spices, and soon a gigantic spice trade began.

The Venetians and Genoese contributed ships already to the First Crusade. In return, the new Christian kingdom of Jerusalem gave them full rights of future trade along its coasts, especially at Tyre and Sidon. When Venice saw how the Byzantine wholesalers raised the price of spices, she started her own Crusade, the Fourth. It proved a disaster for Constantinople, which—like Crete—continued to act as an important Venetian colony and trading post for a long time thereafter.

Hop was one of the spices that thirsty Europeans prized most highly during the Middle Ages.

Status symbols

The spice trade's attractiveness was due to several factors: it was lucrative, spices could be transported easily, and vast amounts of them were consumed—although chiefly by the upper classes. But the reason for so much spice-eating was simply the poor quality of foodstuffs: if not half-rotten, they wallowed in salt, the only preservative suitable for mass production in olden times. Beverages were scarcely better: the wines began to taste like vinegar when shipped abroad in barrels, and home-brewed beer quickly soured.

Advantages of taste were supplemented by the thought of status. Expensive spices meant that it was "high class" to make food and drink as spicy as possible. This idea had odd results, such as gingerbread and mulled wine.

An example of "spice frenzy" at the peak of the Middle Ages comes from the fringe of European culture. In 1328, when Birgitta, the national saint of Sweden, held a funeral feast for her father, the bill included 500 grams of cinnamon, 700 of saffron, one kilogram of ginger, three of pepper, five of caraway, and forty of almonds.

Spices and the Renaissance

Until around 1500, the stream of spices followed Arab caravan trails to Constantinople and Alexandria. From there, the spices were shipped to their European destinations in northern Italian vessels. It was almost entirely the spice trade that turned small cities like Genoa and Venice into brilliant metropoli.

And it was the wealth of the spice trade that made possible a great upsurge of culture in northern Italy. Without any exaggeration, one could say that these commercial cities' traffic in spices—through the generosity of the rich people who patronized artists and authors, architects and philosophers—created the Renaissance. Had it not been for them and for spices, we might still be living in the Middle Ages, and would probably be Muslims.

The earth becomes round

But the scene changed rapidly during the fifteenth century. Turkey swallowed the Balkans, made the Black Sea a private pond,

Spice trading in the Renaissance brought great wealth to Naples—shown here in the fourteenth century—just as it did to Genoa and Venice.

and prepared to reach for the Levant and Syria. The old trade routes were cut off, wrecking the spice monopoly of Italian ports such as Venice. Western Europe gave birth to dynamic states along the Atlantic, which were not satisfied to serve as mere retailers of spices and silk. They wanted either to govern the producing countries or, at least, to get the products from their sources.

The new view of the world as a sphere, with the ocean as a passageway—instead of a moat around a flat earth—favoured the ports in countries such as Portugal, Spain, England, France and the Netherlands. Now began the amazing era in Western history that, fueled by spices, changed Europe from an outcrop of the Asian continent into a global power-centre, which it had never been before. The hunt for spices, and for trade routes to where they grew, drove great "discoverers" onto the seas in the sixteenth century.

Perhaps the high point of world commercial history was May 20, 1498, when the Portuguese sailor Vasco da Gama stepped ashore at Calicut in western India. The spice trade, and international maritime traffic as a whole, were instantly transformed. We shall see the consequences in the following pages about different spices and their producers.

From plant to test-tube?

Today, of course, the chemical industry has started to gnaw its way into the spice stores. But we can hope that it will be a long time before natural aromatics are replaced by artificial ones—vanilla is an example of the fact that chemists can succeed rather well. And spices are still an important source of income for the developing countries in which many of them grow. Indeed, the whole economy of some lands is at the mercy of the price of a spice. A tiny island nation such as Grenada could hardly exist without controlling a third of the world's nutmeg production, besides a fat share of its clove farms.

When the Portuguese seafarer Vasco da Gama arrived at Calicut on the western coast of India in 1498, it meant that Portugal had beaten Spain in the struggle for the spice market. But the Spanish could hardly complain, as they had Columbus...

Spices for everyone?

There is also a social aspect to the history of spices, apart from geography. They have not only wandered between countries, but are links between classes of people. European food tastes in the past show a development of fashions in cooking. From the Italian kitchen with its roots in classical Rome arose the modern French style, and from Germany a number of culinary trends spread to the royalty of neighbouring countries during the sixteenth century. With time, French cuisine has become a heritage of the Western world.

These novelties did not, however, sink very deep into the minds of the masses. The peasants, a majority of all Europeans even in the early part of our century, were scarcely affected by shifts in upper-class taste. They primarily used the herbs that could be produced at home; imported spices were usually much too expensive for ordinary people.

The export product of Grenada, the "nutmeg island": fruit, aril and seed.

In the seventeenth century, "ordinary" townsfolk could not afford to use large amounts of imported spices. Here a bourgeois wife crushes some home-grown spices in her mortar.

Culinary technology—or rather the lack of it, in most homes—did little to promote a more elaborate spice culture. The common man cooked in the kitchen's sole pot, mixing meat or fish with whatever vegetables were available: mostly various sorts of cabbage and root crops. The old traditional spices suited them nicely. Yet meat was roasted on a spit only in richer homes, and not until the nineteenth century did new types of stoves and kitchen equipment become widespread. It was then that the nobility's exotic spices began to play a general role in the eating habits of entire populations.

Europe's own herbs

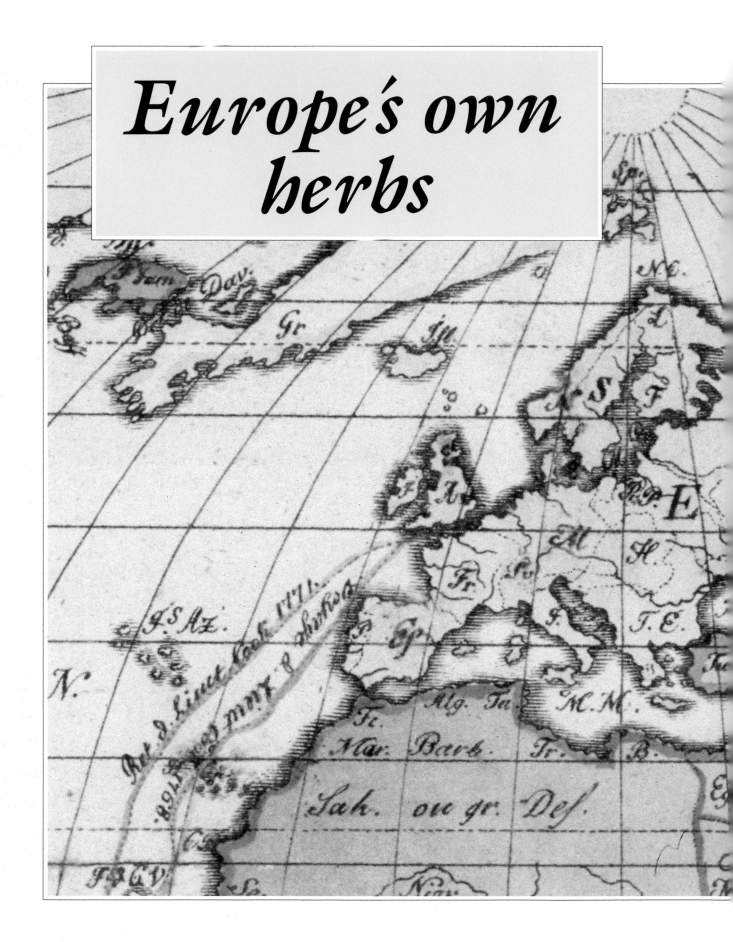

A classical heritage

The roots of modern natural science stretch back to the cultures of ancient Greece and Rome. Until that time, people's relationship to other living things—such as plants—must have been determined mainly by their practical needs. Plants provided them with raw foods, healing remedies, materials for equipment and so on. Knowledge of how to use plants was passed on by verbal tradition from one generation to the next. When deep questions arose about the world's origin, function and destiny, the answers were given by religion and mythology, which placed human beings in the broad perspective of a cosmos controlled by higher powers.

The dawn of spice science

A theoretical view of nature, in Western lands, was first established primarily by Aristotle and his philosophical school in Athens. But the purpose of bringing mankind and its own life into focus continued for a long while. Astronomy is perhaps the clearest example of this attitude—yet the biological environment was also studied chiefly in terms of usefulness for man. Plants seemed to be a treasure-trove of public utilities, no less important for medicine than for economics.

One of Aristotle's pupils, Theophrastus, was a pioneer of botanical literature. Around 300 B.C., he wrote the two oldest known works on botany in our civilization. His *Inquiry into Plants* led to a field of authorship that has flourished for over 2,000 years—"herbal" books. In them, botany and medicine went hand in hand. Much of their specific advice about plants and remedies was based on theories developed by the "father of

John Gerard's famous Herball, *published in 1597, paid homage even on its title page to his ancient Greek predecessors, Theophrastus and Dioscorides. This pioneering book catalogued over 1,000 species of plants, including many spices.*

medicine", Hippocrates, in about 400 B.C.

Among these ideas was "humoral pathology". Sickness and health, it taught, depended on a balance between four fluids in the body: blood, phlegm, black and yellow bile. A healthy person was "of sound humour", and a patient's balance could be restored with blood-letting, enemas, laxatives and emetics. Physicians and botanists then fitted plants into this system—by classifying them as cold or warm, dry or moist. Such was the origin of many prescriptions that made use of plants in later centuries.

Magic in the garden

Alongside those learned doctrines, though, other concepts of a far more primitive kind existed. To begin with, medicinal plants were often employed together with superstitions, strange to our minds—spells and rituals which, in Christian times, were replaced to some extent by prayers for the help of Jesus, Mary, various saints and apostles. Such aids to therapy could, of course, have great value for people who believed in them, reinforcing the "placebo" effect of a cure. Today we can feel this suggestive power of medicine as soon as the doctor takes out his pen to write a prescription.

In addition, the world was thought to have magical or supranormal aspects—generally because of superficial resemblances between quite different things. Traditional doctors and botanists systematized these aspects. Thus, for instance, a plant's similarity to a bodily organ was seen as nature's instruction about how it should be used. Hepatica, whose leaves recall the three lobes of the liver, acquired a reputation for curing liver ailments; it was an approved pharmaceutical in Denmark as late as 1772.

From devil's dung to perfume

More spectacular peculiarities of a plant were also important in medical botany. If it had flowers or leaves with a sharp, bitter taste, an odd shape or an unusual way of growing, such circumstances stimulated the imagination: it was sure to possess some hidden power which could benefit humans. The prominent roles of mistletoe and rowan in magic, and in folk medicine, reflect their curious ability to grow up on other trees.

Likewise, a resin named asafetida (from the Eastern plant *Ferula asafoetida*), was used widely as a remedy, and by old-fashioned veterinarians even in our century. This certainly owed to the stink which it produced, also being known as "devil's dung". And anything that smelled so awful simply had to work medical wonders!

With time, people lost faith in herbs which obviously had no such powers. Yet many famous medicines of the past continued to be served as spices. Their tastes had become familiar, and they found a place in the kitchen instead of the pharmacy. A perfect example is the plant that provides asafetida. Both its root resin and other parts are a popular aid to cooking, halfway between a vegetable and a

Pharmacies such as this one from about 1800 sold a great range of medicinal herbs, many of which are used today as spices.

spice, in India and Iran, notably for meatballs and pickles. In Europe and America, the plant has survived in the perfume industry.

The strong and the soft

A common feature of many European spices is that their aroma is mild and derives, to a large extent, from their leaves. There are some fierce exceptions, whose taste is due to their seeds (as with mustard) or underground parts (such as onions and horseradish). These have held a traditional place as everyday spices at our tables. Still, the sophisticated leaf-spices are most prominent when it comes to the fine art of ultramodern restaurant cuisine—and when we try to impress our guests with cooking that draws, in particular, on the experience of southern Europe.

Mustard

Sinapis alba, Brassica nigra

Once there were two farmers who had just done good business at the horse-market in town. Excited by the jingle of money in their pockets, they decided to celebrate at the main hotel. Sitting around the table next to theirs was a group of city-folk. They watched how these fine gentlemen took something yellow from a small can and laid it on pieces of meat before filling their mouths. It must be very expensive, the farmers agreed, since so little of it was used. "That's what we'll eat today," said one to the other, "we can afford it!" A party had to be a party, and a stylish party as well.

So when a waiter came to get their orders, they asked for the yellow stuff—whatever it was. And not such a small can's worth, but a whole plateful for each of them. Soon they were shovelling it into themselves, but their eyes began to run, and their gums burned like fire. In the end they both exclaimed that high-class food was nothing for honest people!

A spice for nobles

This fictitious tale, recorded in Estonia, was related chiefly by the urban nobility, to make fun of the peasants. Yet like most folklore, it contains a seed of truth. Newly rich horse-traders were by no means alone in their unfamiliarity with mustard. Though we may consider it the commonest of all spices—apart from salt and sugar—mustard did not initially exist on the local farmers' tables.

The use of mustard as a spice belongs to the many culinary innovations which started in the ancient Mediterranean cultures. At first, however, mustard was regarded mainly as a medicinal plant. The Greek scientist Pythagoras, in the sixth century B.C., declared mustard to be an excellent cure for scorpion-bites. Perhaps he was following the principle that "evil drives out evil", but mustard does yield a powerful skin irritant. A hundred years later, his colleague Hippocrates prescribed

Species name:	Sinapis alba, white mustard
Family:	Brassicaceae (formerly Cruciferae), mustard and cabbage plants
Spicy part:	Seeds (the leaves are also used as salad)
Origin:	Mediterranean countries
Cultivation:	USA, Canada, Denmark, Germany, Holland, France, Britain, China and Japan
Common names:	French: moutarde German: Senf Italian: senape Spanish: mostaza Swedish: senap

Species name:	Brassica nigra, black mustard
Family:	Brassicaceae (formerly Cruciferae), mustard and cabbage plants
Spicy part:	Seeds (the leaves are also used as salad)
Origin:	Mediterranean countries
Cultivation:	In most countries; exported notably by USA and Chile
Common names:	French: moutarde German: Senf Italian: senape Spanish: mostaza Swedish: senap

a wide range of decocts made with mustard.

In Rome, the scientist Pliny the Elder, during the first century after Christ, announced that lazy women would turn into ideal housewives if they were fed mustard. At the same time, mustard became a part of Roman meals. The famous cookbook by a gourmet named Apicius employed mustard as a spice for various recipes, not least in the form of mustard sauce. There were sauces including mustard for boiled birds such as ostrich, crane and duck, fried doves, boiled boar and other game, pig teats, and several fish dishes. As at our own hot-dog stands, Apicius also served mustard on boiled sausage.

Spreading mustard

Mustard passed from Rome to other countries like France. In Charlemagne's age— the ninth century A.D.— mustard was cultivated by, for example, the imperial estates and the many monastery gardens near Paris. The Roman tradition of mustard sauces can be said to survive in a classic of French cuisine, the *sauce Robert*. This occurs in cookbooks as far back as the seventeenth century, with its basic ingredients of mustard and onions. French mustard gave rise to both superb cooking and an important side-industry, notably in Bourgogne where Dijon is the "mustard capital" today.

Mustard is usually thought to have reached Germany and England during the twelfth century. Whether it arrived in Spain and Portugal with the Romans, or later with the Arabs, is uncertain. Still, Vasco da Gama took a barrel of mustard on his voyage to India.

Why call it mustard?

It is from France that West European words such as *moutarde* derive. Two explanations have been given. A fanciful one is that Duke Philip the Bold placed a motto, *Moult Me*

Mustard's taste is released only when the seeds are crushed and the powder is mixed with water.

Tarde, on the coat-of-arms which he granted to Dijon in 1382. The city's mustard-makers set the motto on their cans, but they were bad at spelling, so it became *Moutarde*. According to etymologists, though, *moutarde* is a contraction of *mustum ardens*, the medieval Latin for "hot wine must"—because mustard was made in Burgundy with the help of grape must, or possibly wine-vinegar.

Some other European names for mustard are due to the Latin *sinapis*, of which we know only that it must have reached Rome via Greece from Egypt. It lives on in the Italian *senape*, and its descendants in most Germanic languages show how mustard, too, spread from Roman kitchens to northern ones during the early Middle Ages. A curious exception is that, in medieval Norway, the spice was termed *mustardhr* — obviously borrowed then from either English or French. This suggests an unfamiliarity with mustard, and the term did occur in texts that seem to be literary loans or translations. Thus a "mustard frontier" in culinary customs apparently ran across southern Scandinavia.

The politics of mustard

Denmark had an advanced culture with close links to the rest of the Continent. Ordinary Danes imitated their nobles in eating mustard, and continued to do so even where they were conquered by the Swedes. But in most of northern Europe, the habit long remained a luxury of the ruling classes, which the peasant masses did not bother to copy. It was therefore easy for the high to ridicule the low with "mustard anecdotes" like the one already mentioned.

The first time that Norwegians definitely made an acquaintance with mustard, violence was involved. Some idle Vikings settled on the Isle of Man and found it boring. In the year 1234, they heard that the Orkney Islands had fallen into a state of anarchy, and sailed there for plunder. But another tough

A flowering field of mustard is a colourful sight, as seen here in southern Sweden.

customer, the Earl of Conway, arrived beforehand and captured them. Each was drowned by being placed upside-down in a separate barrel of mustard. This method of execution has, to my knowledge, never been used before or since.

Folklore about mustard

Odd beliefs have long been associated with this spice. In Germany it is said that, if a bride sews mustard seeds into her wedding gown, she can be sure of "wearing the pants" in her family. Two places as different as Denmark and India illustrate another tradition: evil spirits can be kept out of a house if mustard seeds are strewn around it. Danes also used to mix the seeds with ginger and spearmint, feed the blend to a frigid woman, and expect her to change her ways. In the Faeroe Islands, toothaches were cured by smearing the cheek with a "mustard plaster" made from the powder—one of the oldest roles played by such plants in folk medicine.

Varieties of mustard

Mustard is a collective name for several cruciferous (cross-shaped) plants, some of which are related to cabbages. Most important are the species *Sinapis alba* and *Brassica nigra*. The terms "white" (or yellow) and "black" (or brown) mustard are often applied to these two, respectively.

As a rule, the prepared mustard we buy in stores—like the "English" mustard powder we make our own variants with—consists of white mustard, perhaps yellowed by an additive such as turmeric. The product's taste can be improved by adding (besides water) vinegar or wine-vinegar, sugar and salt. It can even be seasoned with honey, garlic, tarragon and much else. Black mustard is commonest in local "peasant" varieties of mustard, notably in France and Sweden.

Points of caution

Mustard is a peculiar spice, in that its taste develops only after the seeds are crushed and their powder is mixed with water. Two substances, from different types of cells, then

Sewing mustard seeds into a wedding gown is an old German tradition, meant to ensure the wife's authority in the family.

come into contact: sinigrin and myrosin. The resultant "mustard oil" has the slightly sour, but primarily pungent, taste that we expect of mustard. About 10-15 minutes are needed for the mixture to reach its full aroma. Home-made mustard should thus be prepared around half an hour before serving it. Subsequently the taste fades a little, so there is no point in making more than a day's worth at a time.

The development can be delayed or stopped with an additive like vinegar, wine vinegar or lemon juice. Ready-mixed mustard is always seasoned with such an acid. This should not be done to mustard for immediate use or for a sauce, but most people add the acid because their tongues are accustomed to it by commercial mustards. Alas, it prevents the full taste of mustard from emerging!

Whether or not to add sugar is a controversial matter. I myself enjoy some sweetness in mustard, ideally from honey—a combination that is thousands of years old. However, taste is admittedly individual. Why not experiment, the next time you mix mustard for your sausage, instead of taking a detour with the standard blends from factories? And when mustard is used in sauces, to change its basic taste is a serious error, since its acidity or sweetness goes into the sauce and can ruin your dream-dish.

Uncrushed mustard seeds are widely employed in preserving, for example, sauerkraut and pickles in vinegar. They do not give any typical "mustard sting" to these foods, but simply impart a fine, mild aroma.

Calf kidneys in mustard sauce

*M*ost mustard is spread on dishes ready for eating, such as sausage and other meats. Nobody needs a recipe for this, but it helps to know that the mustard which goes with boiled fish is not so good on sausage. A well-stocked pantry contains several kinds: fish mustard, light and dark French wine-vinegar mustard (for dressings and such), an unsweetened (for sauces) and a very sharp mustard of English type.

But mustard is also a good spice to cook with. Among the dishes to which it is often added are kidneys, as is illustrated by the "sautéed calf kidneys with three sorts of mustard" which a famous French chef, Raymond Oliver, launched. Here is a simpler variant:

*B*egin by rinsing and drying the kidneys. Cut them in centimetre-thick slices, then cut away unwanted fat. With lamb kidneys, the slices should be soaked in milk for an hour or two. After spicing with salt and pepper, fry the slices quickly in a fairly hot pan—they should become pink inside, but have a well-browned surface. Next, pour the cognac over them, light the gravy with a match, and shake the pan a little while it flames. When the fire is out, lay the kidney pieces in a heated deep dish or foil to keep them warm. Whip the mustard into the gravy, dilute it with cream, let it boil until rather thick, and season with salt and pepper. You can enrich the aroma with an herbal blend or a dash of Worcester-shire sauce. Place the kidney slices on a well-heated serving-dish and pour on the sauce. Having already fried the bacon, break it up over the dish. Strew on a little chopped parsley. Serve with rice or mashed potatoes. A good side-treat is white bread fried in butter.

> ## INGREDIENTS
>
> *1 calf (or lamb) kidney, per two people*
>
> *1.5 dl (10 tbsp) thick cream*
>
> *3–4 tablespoons cognac*
>
> **Butter for frying**
>
> **Salt and pepper (possibly herbal)**
>
> *4 slices of crisp-fried bacon*
>
> **Finely chopped parsley**

Hop

Humulus lupulus

At the time of Alexander the Great, in the fourth century before Christ, lived a man named Pytheas. Born in the Greek colony where we now find the French port of Marseilles, he made history as the first known traveller from the south to the distant north of Europe. While visiting England, he heard rumours of a remarkable land even farther north, beyond icy and misty seas. Its inhabitants were said to produce not wine, but a drink consisting of grain and honey. This custom, odd to a Greek, impressed Pytheas so much that it played a leading role in his pioneering account of the region —probably a part of Scandinavia—which was to be called "Ultima Thule".

Describing the Germanic peoples a few centuries later, Julius Caesar told that they lived on meat, cheese and butter, but preferred to drink up their grain instead of baking bread from it. Not long afterward, the Roman historian Tacitus wrote a famous work on the same peoples, noting with surprise that "for drink they use a liquid made of barley or wheat and, by fermentation, given a certain likeness to wine."

These examples show two things: the Germans were already drinking beer two thousand years ago, and the Romans were not. The latter's neglect of beer is rather curious in a wider perspective. Certainly this drink is an age-old means of making life on earth more bearable. In the Near East, techniques of brewing were apparently invented during prehistoric times. Exactly where and when the first beer soothed a Stone Age throat is, of course, a mystery—yet the early cultures of Egypt and Babylon emerged from obscurity with their goblets full of foaming beer, and it was brewed according to fairly modern methods. Beer brewers can boast the world's oldest industrial branch of chemical engineering, although perhaps together with bakers; the two industries are, indeed, closely related in terms of their raw materials and fermentation processes.

The art of spicing beer

In northern Europe, beer has long been the main drink for both festive and ordinary occasions. Thanks to the prehistoric habit of burying the dead along with vessels of food and drink, in case they should end up at a place of few refreshments, our archaeologists have been able to detect the dried remains of beer on potsherds. The beer was evidently spiced, as a rule, with aromatic or mildly bitter herbs. In Scandinavia these were often sweet-gale, yarrow, marsh tea, meadowsweet, cowslip or wormwood; on the Continent, juniper berries and tree bark among others.

Spices that enhanced a feeling of drunkenness in beverages were naturally most popular, but some of them must have been harmful—as for example

Species name:	*Humulus lupulus*
Family:	*Cannabaceae, the hemp plants*
Spicy part:	*The female plant's cone-like fruit formation*
Origin:	*Temperate areas of Eurasia and North America; first cultivated in eastern Europe*
Cultivation:	*USA, Germany (each with 30% of world production), Czechoslovakia*
Common names:	*French:* *houblon* *German:* *Hopfen* *Italian:* *luppolo* *Spanish:* *lúpolo* *Swedish:* *humle*

Humulus lupulus. ♀
Humle. Kyrkhult, Blk.
a. Honblomma, förstorad
b. Fruktställning ell. kotte
c. Tvenne honblommor med stödjeblad. och förblad
Ch. v. el. e 1905.

Hop plants grow to a considerable height. Once there was a small hop garden on nearly every farm, sometimes required by law. Today, cultivation on a large scale supplies the beer breweries.

when beer was laced with henbane, the "weed of witches". The same is still more true of a much-discussed beer additive, the red mushroom known as fly agaric (its white cousin, the "death-cap", is never drunk twice!). This contains a drug which, if taken in some quantity, has a powerful inebriating effect. People intoxicated with it become aggressive and violent. There is a theory that the Scandinavian Vikings who became notorious fighters with the title of "berserks" drank beer spiced with fly agaric to put themselves in the right frame of mindlessness.

This strange sort of beer has also been enjoyed in some other parts of northern Europe and Asia. It was once reported from Siberia that the urine of men who had consumed beer spiced with fly agaric was drunk by their wives, who thus shared a bit of their gladness, as the intoxicating substances did not entirely disappear while passing through their bodies. A late instance of berserk Scandinavians occurred during the last war fought by Sweden—against Norway in 1814. Officers coming from Stockholm reported with amazement how a number of tough lads in a local regiment chewed fly agaric before going into battle, and (understandably) they won.

The versatile value of hop

But already in the early Middle Ages, beer-drinking Europe got to know the new spice which, ever since then, has been inextricably linked with the brewing of beer. Hop is a plant that grows wild, or has become wild, throughout much of temperate Eurasia and North America. Its fruit formation, resembling a cone, develops small yellow glandules that secrete a sticky substance called lupulin. This contains several bitter components, such as lupulon and humulon, which have a wonderful impact on beer. They help to preserve it (formerly a big problem), make it more foamy, and give it the special bitter taste that characterizes any good beer. However, lupulin also has medicinal effects that were a factor in the medieval history of hop.

Dried hop cones.

Hop was cultivated by the Greeks and Romans, but only as a medicinal herb and a vegetable. Its fresh shoots were eaten like asparagus—as was also done, for instance, in Denmark and Holland as late as the eighteenth century. People soon discovered that its glandules had slightly narcotic properties; and during our own time Englishmen, in particular, have smoked hops in about the same manner as opium. Danish soldiers fighting a war against Germany in 1864 found that their tobacco was giving out, so they crushed dry hop cones and stuffed these into their cigarettes. This substitute was occasionally tried even during the Second World War, being said to taste better if the hops were mixed with cherry leaves.

Others have been content to put hop cones in their bed-pillows, as a measure against insomnia. Medicinally, hop has been considered to promote sleep as well as to stimulate the appetite. This may seem contradictory, but the chief claim for hop has always been its calming effect on "irritations in the sexual organs", as we read in old encyclopedias. Yet the value of hop as a beer spice, not as a medicine, was what surely endeared it to the hearts of some Turkish, Finno-Ugric and Slavic peoples, along the Volga River and later to the south and east of the Baltic Sea.

The first hop farms

For the modern use of hop did come from the east, and is thought to have reached central Europe already in the sixth century. The earliest known hop farm, in the year 736, lay in Bavaria—where the cultivation of hop was supposedly introduced by Slavic prisoners of war during the seventh century. Thirty years afterward, hop was farmed at the famous, influential monastery of Saint-Gall in Switzerland. It also graced the French court of Pepin the Younger in 768. Hop as a beer spice probably came to Scandinavia only when adopted by the monasteries, but the plant is likely to have been grown there previously for textiles (it is a distant relative of hemp).

Monasteries were undoubtedly the agency through which hop triumphed over all the other traditional beer-spices. Its victory was due, not least, to its reputed countereffect on sexuality—an obvious advantage for monks, and a definite contrast to the powers which were once ascribed to many Oriental spices.

The hop harvest in former times was also an entertaining social occasion—not least for young people—when work could be combined with play in traditional country life. This scene was painted in 1856 by the Swedish artist Wilhelm Wallander.

Cultivating hop

Hop is a trailing plant that winds clockwise around tree trunks or other supports, and clings to them with its tiny crossbow-like barbs. The Romans believed, quite wrongly, that a hop plant sucked the life out of the trees it climbed on. They called it "little wolf", which is the meaning of the second word in its species name, *Humulus lupulus.*

A growth of hops is a unique sight: the plants are 6-7 metres high and need very tall poles to climb on, giving the hop-yard a characteristic appearance. And in all the Scandinavian countries, for example, the peasants were once required to grow a certain minimum number of hops in their gardens: 30 in Denmark (from the year 1446), and no fewer than 200 in Sweden (from 1474), al-though only six hop-poles per farm in Norway (from 1490).

Hop is a dioecious plant, the male and female flowers growing separately. The female flowers sit in tight, cone-like formations, while the male formations are strongly divided. The leaves are opposed and palmate. Wild hop is often found along riverbanks, but has a much lower content of lupulin than do the refined, cultivated varieties. Hops can grow well in loose, limy soil and a rather damp climate. A hop plant is very productive for 15-20 years, and is harvested in August-September, when the cones turn a yellow-green to yellow-brown colour. The plants are carefully pulled down from their supports and taken home to the farm for picking.

The final reward of hop: beer ready to be tasted.

Life among cones

Hop-picking was once a great pleasure of country life, as narrated for instance by Hans Christian Andersen. Both adults and children participated, and the work was fairly quiet, allowing them to tell stories and sing while they laboured. Once all the hop-bines were free of cones, it was time—at least for the grownups—to have a hop party.

The cones are then dried for 4-5 days, and should be shaken and turned in the meantime. They are sensitive and must be handled with care during their onward journey to the brewery. There, when the wort has been filtered out of the mash-pans, it is boiled for a couple of hours together with the hops, which yield their useful and tasteful substances. Depending on the desired strength of hops, between 100 and 400 grams are added to every 100 litres of wort.

World annual production of hops is around 125,000 tons, which are grown on more than 90,000 hectares of land. Formerly the other parts of the hop plant were exploited as well: its leaves were gladly eaten by livestock, and the stem fibres could be used to make yarn for rope or coarse cloths such as hop-sack.

Wormwood

Artemisia absinthium

In ancient Rome, many public festivals were held during the year. One of them, known as the Latin Feast, included a chariot race on the Capitoline Hill. The winners were given a glass of wormwood wine, which was thought to be an appropriate prize because it conveyed good health. From this ceremony a long tradition has continued down to our time—resulting not only in the drink called vermouth, but also in various bitters and snaps which rely on wormwood for their taste.

An old life-saver

But the medical value of common wormwood was not a Roman discovery. It played a role in the oldest of all medical books, the Papyrus Ebers, written in Egypt 3,500 years ago. Several of the classic Greek and Roman works on medicine stated that wormwood could promote digestion, bowel movement and sexual life. One can hardly demand more of such an ordinary drug! Although the great physician Galen considered wormwood wine to be mainly an emetic to induce vomiting, its reputation grew. The idea that wormwood eliminated "stomach worms" gave rise to its name in English and several other languages.

Into the kitchen

Gradually, however, the plant's culinary features came to outweigh its

Species name:...........Artemisia absinthium		
Family:...................Asteraceae (Compositae), the composite plants		
Spicy part:...............Leaves, and sometimes flowers		
Origin:...................Europe in general		
Cultivation:...........Local, but the wild form is considered better		
Common Names:.. French:	absinthe	
German:	Wermut	
Italian:	assenzio	
Spanish:	ajenjo	
Swedish:	malört	

medical ones. Pork and lamb meat were found to be especially improved by putting wormwood leaves in the pot. Turnips could become far more exciting if seasoned with wormwood. This was the most familiar wild spice in Germanic countries, until countless others were introduced by the monasteries.

In addition, a belief arose that the sharp aroma of wormwood was disliked by some animals, not least by pests such as mice and moths. Farmers often tried to protect their seed and grain from rodents by surrounding storehouses with a barrier of wormwood. This was done in parts of Germany as late as the 1930s. Librarians and authors were quite convinced that mice hated wormwood: they mixed its juice into ink, so that their manuscripts would not be eaten up.

A boon to beverages

In spite of these uses, it was chiefly as a spice in drinks that wormwood gained acceptance. The Greek doctor Anthimus noted, in the sixth century, that Germanic peoples enjoyed a wine (probably beer!) flavoured with wormwood. Other ancient writers recorded similar habits in Roman Gaul, where wormwood later served as a drink-spice even in the highest circles. At the Merovingian court of Soissons, King Chilperic I—an unpleasant barbarian—was apparently assassi-

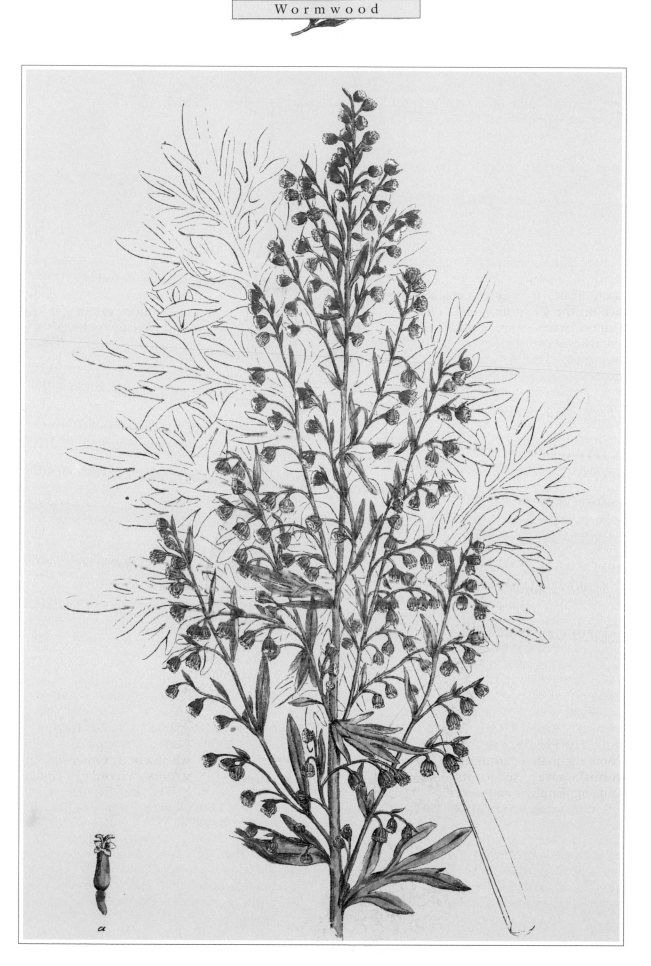

nated with a goblet of poisoned wine, whose taste had been disguised by wormwood and honey. When the technique of distillation, known to Arabs long before the Christians inherited it, was brought by the Saracens into southern France, the local wormwood became one of the spices they used to improve brandy.

Did people think that wormwood tasted good? Perhaps the primary aim was to make its bitterness cover up the frequent bad taste of beer and wine in those days. Beer quickly soured, and the wine that was transported by primitive methods had partly turned into vinegar by the time it reached consumers.

The wine-importing countries in northern Europe had another problem. They learned how to make liquor from grain during the seventeenth century, and from potatoes a hundred years afterward. But with their crude equipment, the drink contained so much of a by-product, fusel oil, that it tasted awful. Strong additives were needed to hide the noxious fumes of such mulled wine. The Scandinavians used wormwood. In England and Holland, where this plant served few purposes, juniper was the chosen spice—leading to the invention of gin and geneva, respectively.

Hidden powers

By contrast, the French preferred to exploit the narcotic effect of a substance in wormwood leaves. The outcome was a liqueur called absinthe (from the plant's Greek and Latin names), which caused mental and physical illness until it was forbidden—by the Swiss in 1907, and later in many other countries.

Vermouth was created in 1786, its name deriving from the German word for wormwood. Its inventor, Antonio Benedetto Carpano of Turin, supposedly got the latter idea from his reading of Goethe's works. Today, the drink is seasoned with a dozen different spices, wormwood being an unimportant one.

Plants and substances with a pungent aroma have long been thought to keep away evil spirits. A well-known example is garlic, but similar qualities have been ascribed to wormwood in many parts of Europe. Its rich

Absinthe, a drink made with the help of wormwood, was associated during the late nineteenth century with decadent poets and proletarian misery—as in the famous painting "L'Absinthe" (1876) by Edgar Degas.

folklore includes protection against the "evil eye" and other curses. Even in Vietnam, a related species once had the reputation of repelling demons.

Wormwood in nature

Common wormwood is a perennial, growing up to 1.5 metres tall. While native to Europe, it has been spread to North America. Herbs and shrubs of the same large genus *Artemisia*, generally termed wormwoods, are widely distributed and include some other spices such as tarragon.

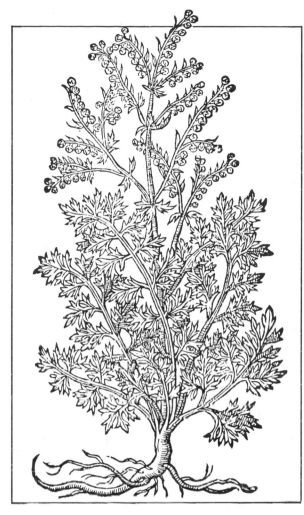

Wormwood had been well-known for thousands of years before it appeared in this woodcut, from the Danish botanist Simon Paulli's Flora Danica *(1648).*

As a whole, this plant is conspicuously downy-grey. Belonging to the composite-flowered family, it has small dome-shaped clusters along the stalk branches, with yellow tube-like edge-flowers and funnel-like disk-flowers. These appear in August, and are usually harvested just before they die.

The wild species Artemisia maritima, *related to common wormwood, is also popular in Scandinavia as a spice for liquors.*

Laurel

Laurus nobilis

Apollo, the ancient Greek god of music, prophecy, and the sun, once quarrelled with his father. Zeus became furious, and banished the lad from Mount Olympus to live among mortals. There he had a difficult time, though he managed to seduce a fair number of earthly beauties. Despite his own charm, not all of them submitted.

According to our sources, one of the nymphs who hunted with the goddess Artemis, named Daphne, was definitely hard to catch. Falling in love with her, Apollo noticed that he had a rival—young Leucippus, who dressed up as a nymph in order to be near Daphne. Apollo persuaded the nymphs to go swimming, whereupon they discovered the true sex of Leucippus and killed him. Finally Apollo went after Daphne, but she fled and appealed to her father, the river-god Peneios, to save her maidenhood. He changed her into a laurel tree, and the sequel was told by the Roman poet Ovid in *Metamorphoses*:

> "Then the god said,
>   So be it!
> If you can't become
>   my wife,
> you'll still remain my
>   tree;
> I shall always carry the
>   laurel,
> eternally adorn with you
> my hair, my lyre and
>   quiver."

This was meant to explain the fact that laurel trees were considered to be sacred to Apollo.

Species name:.........	*Laurus nobilis*
Family:.................	*Lauraceae, laurel plants*
Spicy part:.............	*Dried leaves; formerly also berries(drupes)*
Origin:.................	*Near East, Syria*
Cultivation:..........	*Mediterranean countries, especially Italy (leading exporter), Spain, Portugal, Greece and Turkey; Eastern Asia; Central America, notably Guatemala*
Common names:.....	*French: laurier* *German: Lorbeer, Suppenblätter* *Italian : alloro* *Spanish: laurel* *Swedish: lager*

A potent symbol

However, the god's connection with laurel may have been of a less religious, and more botanical, kind. People who slept on a bed of laurel twigs, and inhaled their spicy vapour, supposedly had dreams that came true. At Delphi, the home of Apollo's most famous oracle, laurel trees played an important role for the prophetess. Whoever received a happy answer from her was crowned with a laurel wreath. Such wreaths became symbols of victory in the local athletic games, ancestral to the Olympics. Eventually they signified military triumph—but when the Roman Senate gave Caesar permission to wear one, its main purpose was to disguise his baldness.

Since Apollo was the patron of fine arts, his laurel eventually served to show that great poets had won his favour. Even today in Britain, there is a royally appointed "poet laureate". Opera singers and other performers may be celebrated with a laurel wreath around their necks. Some scientists have earned the same honour. The academic title "baccalaureate" is loosely associated with the laurel, which thus became an emblem of graduation from universities in several countries. The Latin for laurel berries, *baca lauri*, gave rise to the French word *baie*. This has led us to speak of "bay leaves" as a spice, although "bay" is also applied to various other plants.

From darkest prehistory

Laurus nobilis Linn.

onward, the laurel has been credited with magical properties. One of these is protection against lightning; in fact the Roman emperor Tiberius, when he heard thunder, crawled under his bed with a laurel wreath on his head. Not long afterward, Nero escaped into a laurel grove during a plague, which was thought to be afraid of the tree.

A place in old pots

Gastronomic traditions about laurel are as ancient as its cultural ones. Both its berries and leaves were regarded as indispensable spices by Apicius in a Roman cookbook of the first century A.D. They were exported to northern Europe quite early in the Middle Ages, and appeared often in books of herbal medicine. Evidently their chief use at this time was for healing —as when Charlemagne encouraged the planting of laurel groves in his realm. For example, ailments of the stomach, kidneys and skin (including acne) were treated with laurel.

The traditional bouquet garni *is tied with parsley, laurel and thyme. Such clusters of spice herbs can be conveniently added to the cooking-pot according to taste.*

In 1652, François-Pierre de la Varenne published one of the truly classic cookbooks, *Le Cuisinier Français*. Laurel leaves belonged to his arsenal of spices. He may well have learned about them when, as a young man, he studied Italian cuisine in Florence. Before

The myth of Daphne's transformation into a laurel tree in order to preserve her purity was once a favourite theme in works of art. Here the sad end of Apollo's courtship is portrayed in a French manuscript of Ovid's Metamorphoses *(c. 1450).*

Maria de Medici moved to France as the wife of King Henry IV, she made sure that cooks would be there who could prepare edible—that is, Italian—food. For the French were not yet renowned chefs, and Maria was a real gourmet.

At the brilliant court of the Medici, old traditions of cooking were carried on. And the recipes obtained by Varenne, once adapted to his country's taste, laid the foundation for the French cuisine that was to conquer the world. His book is also a milestone in the history of spices. Originally, people used spices primarily to compensate for the poor quality of foods, and therefore had to use plenty of them. But Varenne introduced their new role: bringing out the intrinsic taste of the food.

The mild, yet distinctive, aroma of laurel leaves fitted such a role perfectly. Indeed, northern Italy is still one of the world's main suppliers of this spice. It now has very wide applications, from marinades to all sorts of meat stews, fricassees and fish dishes. The whole leaves are almost always used, and they form part of the classic French *bouquet garni* which bubbles in many bouillons, sauces and soups —invented by a contemporary of Varenne, named Pierre de Lune, who was chef to the Duke of Orleans. Laurel leaves are a must in any bouillabaisse, and old-fashioned cookbooks even add them to some puddings and desserts, an odd habit to our minds.

An attractive plant

Eternally green, the laurel begins as a pyramid-shaped bush and grows into a tree at

least 10 metres—and not seldom 20 metres—tall. Its leaves are dark-green, lanceolate and fairly hard, with lighter and less shiny undersides. The bark is soft, either olive-green or reddish. Little yellow or greenish-white flowers, both male and female, spring from the tree's leaf folds. The shiny berries (drupes) are the size of small grapes or cherries, and may be green, purple or black.

Laurel leaves and berries contain essential oils which give them a bitter, spicy taste: eugenol, cineol and geraniol. From the berries is pressed a thick oil, once rather popular in medicine (as a liniment, for instance) and technology (for soap and candles).

The leaves are picked by hand, early in the morning, and then laid to dry—preferably under light pressure to minimize curling. If dried in the sun, they would lose much of their aroma and also become brown.

Laurel belongs to a plant family rich in spices. Among them are cinnamon and cassia. The areas where laurel is cultivated today are similar in climate to its original homeland in Asia Minor. A closely related species grows abundantly in the Canary Islands.

But laurel should not be confused with plants that, while resembling it in name and some qualities, are classified differently by botanists. An example is the cherry laurel, *Prunus laurocerasus*, a poisonous member of the rose family. This evergreen occurs in gardens much farther north than the genuine laurel.

Onions

Onion, Garlic, Chive & Leek

The Greek author Herodotus travelled widely in the middle of the fifth century B.C., so as to give a correct account of the wars between his country, Persia, Egypt and other lands, which were the main subject of his famous *History*. He not only saw the places involved, but described his experiences and what he heard about the exotic customs of foreign peoples. Standing before the Pyramids, as amazed as a modern tourist, he was given a translation of the hieroglyphs on the great monument of Cheops, and reported:

"Here it is recorded how much black radish, red onion and garlic went to the workers. I remember what my interpreter said—that it cost 1,600 silver talents (about 40 tons of silver). If this is correct, how much might have been spent on their food and clothing, as well as on iron for tools!"

The story was that, when his funds ran out, Cheops put his daughter in a brothel to earn money for the project. She contributed all that he asked, but wanted to be remembered on her own account. She asked every client to give her a stone, besides the usual fee. And these stones, according to the historian, sufficed to build the medium-sized pyramid of the three.

Divine delicacies

We need not, however, believe any more than the Egyptian passion for onion and garlic.

Onion:

Species name:.........Allium cepa
Family:..................Alliaceae (formerly among the
                        Liliaceae)
Spicy part:..............The bulb on the underground
                        part of the stem
Origin:..................Southwest Asia (?)
Cultivation:...........Locally in many countries. Leading
                        exporters are Egypt, Hungary,
                        Bulgaria, Israel, and California
Common names:....French: oignon
                        German: Zwiebel
                        Italian: cipolla
                        Spanish: cebolla
                        Swedish: matlök

Garlic:

Species name:..........Allium sativum
Family:..................Same as onion
Spicy part:..............The bulb's small cloves
Origin:..................Near East (?)
Cultivation:...........Locally in most Mediterranean
                        countries. Also in USA (a leading
                        exporter of dehydrated garlic),
                        Egypt, Hungary, Bulgaria and
                        Taiwan
Common names:....French: ail
                        German: Knoblauch
                        Italian: aglio
                        Spanish: ajo
                        Swedish: vitlök

Chive:

Species name:..........Allium schoenoprasum
Family:..................Same as onion
Spicy part:..............Leaves
Origin:..................Europe and northern Asia
Cultivation:...........Locally in many countries, also as
                        a decorative house-plant
Common names:....French: ciboule (tte), cive (tte)
                        German: Schnittlauch
                        Italian: cipollina
                        Spanish: cebolleta
                        Swedish: gräslök

Leek:

Species name:.........Allium porrum
Family:..................Same as onion
Spicy part:..............Bulb and tender leaf parts
Origin:..................Mediterranean (?)
Cultivation:..........Locally in many countries
Common names:....French: poireau
                        German: Porree (lauch)
                        Italian: porro
                        Spanish: porro
                        Swedish: purjolök

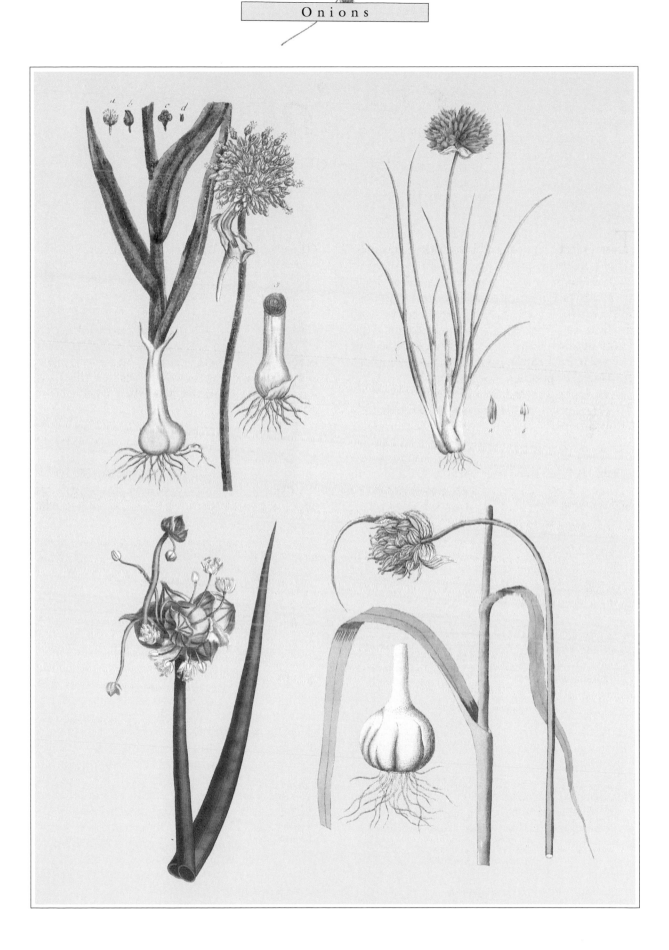

Unlimited supplies of them were evidently a good salary for the hundreds of thousands of poor subjects who raised the Pharaohs' follies.

Another proof of the vegetables' value in the Nile Delta is given by the Bible's book of *Numbers*. The Jews in the desert are said to have grumbled: "We recall the fish that we ate in Egypt, the cucumbers, melons, leeks, red onions and garlic. But now our souls are languishing, for here we have nothing!" It was then that the Lord sent down a rain of manna.

Both garlic and onions can be traced back to 3000 B.C. among the Egyptians, who used them as offerings to the gods and painted them, with botanical clarity, in tombs. The world's oldest known onions, in fact, come from the rich tomb of Tutankhamen, where they were heaped up in 1352 B.C. At sacrifices, onions were elegantly arranged in bell-shaped bunches. However, the priests—according to another Greek, Plutarch, a century after Christ—were not allowed to eat onions. They would have become too thirsty and drunk inappropriate amounts of wine.

Praised in many places

Egyptian onions were renowned for their mild, superb taste. Eaten both cooked and raw, by all classes of society, they may have served as appetizers or side-dishes, much like cabbage. The onions and garlic grown in Egypt and nearby countries are still, to us Westerners, surprisingly mild and crisp.

Ancient Greek onions must also have been good, as Homer compared the fine tunic of his hero Odysseus with an onion's "thin skin". Especially esteemed were those from the isle of Melos (the home of Venus de Milo), which was thus called Krommyusa ("Onion Island").

From further sources, we know that onions and garlic were eaten in huge quantities at the Persian court in Susa. More than 25 kilograms of garlic were consumed there every day, emitting quite an aroma. Cultivation of onions is attested in China since five thousand years ago, and in India since the oldest Vedic writings.

The Egyptians' use of garlic was noted by

Ancient Egypt's tasty onions were mentioned already in the Biblical Book of Numbers. *Onions were commonly offered to the gods and, not surprisingly, were included among the essential grave gifts to be taken to the afterlife.*

yet another Greek author, Charmidas. According to him, men chewed garlic on the way home from their mistresses, so that their jealous wives would not think anyone had come near them. Military experts, such as the Greek Kallias and some Romans, recommended garlic for soldiers before battle—though presumably in order to fire them up, not to repel the enemy with their odour.

Pliny, a later Roman, wrote in his *Natural History* that onions were worth eating because they promoted digestion. He added that "wild onions do not exist": even then, it seems, they were considered to be garden plants. The Romans loved onions, and spread several varieties to the provinces of their empire, including Germany and England.

Red onions and garlic are used primarily as spices, but the somewhat milder yellow onion can be eaten as either a spice or a vegetable.

The travels of onions

But in the Middle Ages, it was the Greek Byzantine Empire that onions made a gastronomic paradise. Emperor Nicephoros II (963-69), a brilliant general, once received a bishop named Liutprand—from Cremona in the Lombard district of northern Italy—as ambassador of the Holy Roman Emperor, Otto the Great of Germany. On returning home, the bishop reported with faint enthusiasm about the Byzantine despot's habits: "He lives on garlic and other onions, washing them down with wine that tastes like bathwater." This was presumably a resinated wine, similar to present-day *retsina* though diluted.

Onions and garlic on people's breath have always bothered their company. Thus Shakespeare, in *A Midsummer Night's Dream,* had Bottom declare:

> "...And, most dear actors,
> eat no onions nor garlic,
> for we are to utter sweet breath..."

It is told that onions were among the first vegetables cultivated by Europeans in the New World. Columbus took onions on his second voyage, and planted them in January 1494 at Isabela, in what is now the Dominican Republic. The Spaniards soon spread them across Central and South America. Even the North American Indians learned from the Europeans to grow onions.

Shallots and leeks

In the same genus as common onions is, for instance, the shallot *(Allium ascalonicum).* This, too, comes from the eastern Mediterranean area. It was named after the city of Ascalon in Palestine, where it was much-cultivated, and apparently the Crusaders took it back to Europe. The local Jews were so fond of onions that Marcus Aurelius, a refined Roman emperor, remarked when he visited their country in the year 175: "O, ye Marcomanni, Quadi and Sarmatians, whom I have just defeated—now I have found a folk that smell even worse!"

Leeks were also familiar in antiquity, and are known to us from the Bible as well as from Egyptian records. The Roman emperor Nero had regular days for eating only leeks with oil. He considered them good for his singing voice—although nothing shows that they helped it, or that his companions liked it. He may have got the idea from Aristotle, as this philosopher claimed that the clear cry of partridge was due to their diet of leeks.

In the British Isles, leeks were especially popular as a food and symbol among the Celtic peoples. An Irish legend told that leeks were created by Saint Patrick. A national dish in Scotland is a soup called "cook-a-leckie". The Welsh used leeks as a national emblem; under King Cadwallader, they wore leeks on their helmets and hoods, to recognize each other during one of their triumphant battles against the Anglo-Saxons in the seventh century. Not unjustifiably, in Shakespeare's play

Onions and their relatives are grown in most vegetable gardens, and there is always some variety that suits the conditions of a particular garden.

Henry V, a comic Welshman named Fluellen was begged to go away because he stank of leeks.

Garlic and chives

Garlic was sold in Greek and Roman cities by wandering merchants. But its odour did not suit the upper classes, and in time it became a proletarian emblem. The poet Horace mentioned it as something which "might fit into the hardened stomachs of harvesters". He reminded his patron Maecenas that, in the legend of the Golden Fleece, the clever Medea had smeared her lover Jason with garlic, so that her father's fire-snorting wild bulls would keep away from him.

Right down to our century, garlic was eaten primarily in Eastern Europe—and among immigrants from there to America. Jewish cuisine made particular use of it. The French were certainly no strangers to its aroma, but treated it carefully: they rubbed the salad bowl with a garlic clove, and some chefs simply breathed over the dish after chewing one. However, since World War II the reputation of garlic has improved enor-

Onion plants are an important source of vitamins, since they can be stored for long periods. These are classic plaits of garlic in a Portuguese shop.

mously, not least because we have learned about exotic kinds of cooking in which garlic is important. Moreover, we have come to realize its health value, even though its medical virtues are often exaggerated.

Chives, with their tender hollow blades, grow wild over much of Europe, northern Asia, and North America—notably around the Great Lakes. They were known as long ago as the Roman poet Martial, who composed an apt epigram: one had to choose between feasting on chives and kissing pretty girls. He preferred the latter, and it was not until the Middle Ages that chives became generally appreciated and cultivated.

Medieval magic

During the early eleventh century, Scandinavia was involved in war between King Canute of Denmark and England, on the one hand, and the Viking leader who was to become the king and national saint of Norway: Olav Haraldsson. In 1030, Olav allied with his Swedish brother-in-law, Anund Jakob, to regain power in Norway, but was beaten at Stiklastad near Trondheim. The

wounded warriors were supposedly brought to a witch-doctoress, who fed onions to those wounded in the stomach. By smelling them, she could soon tell which ones had perforated intestines and would die. Then she was able to concentrate on saving the others.

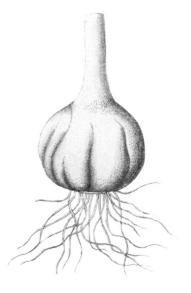

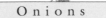

By that time, onions had long been well-known in Norway. Together with garlic, they were probably the most common means of spicing food among the early Scandinavians. Even after the spice trade arrived, particularly with pepper, onions continued to be a daily spice for ordinary folk who could afford nothing else.

All of these plants have been credited with medical and magical qualities, besides their culinary uses and values. The strongest of them, garlic, is surely the best example. What enthusiast of horror-films has not watched garlic holding vampires at bay? Both in ancient and medieval times, garlic was hung around the necks of children to protect them from sorcery. The same was done throughout Europe in the nineteenth-century, although more often with cows and geese. Germans and Czechs even believed that a watch-dog's bite could be made more sharp and painful if it was fed garlic on New Year's Day.

Roots in prehistory

As we can see, the career of such plants began in the mists of time. How they got into our food culture is a controversial issue for botanists. Their original homeland might have been the steppes of western Asia. But the genus *Allium* includes well over a hundred species with varied distribution, and people may have begun to use them at different times and places. Before Europeans reached the New World, bringing along onions, the North American Indians were eating a local relative of garlic, *Allium canadense*.

Two main types of plants are concerned. One has a large, round bulb on its underground stem (onions are not roots!) such as the common white, yellow and red onions. The other has a bulb consisting of several smaller "cloves", as do shallot and garlic. We can also divide the plants according to whether we use the underground bulb or the green parts that grow above the ground—although both are used in the case of leeks.

Chives are an onion plant that grows in the wild. Its mild taste makes it a universal favourite.

Common onions and garlic may be stored for a fairly long time. But the former must first be dried, until their outer blades have hardened to protect the inner ones. Both of these plants are suitable for dehydration and grinding (as in onion salt and garlic powder).

The distinctive aroma of these plants is due to a sulfur-rich, volatile oil. Some of them also contain substances that can kill bacteria or stimulate circulation. This may be worth thinking about, the next time you cry when cutting an onion for a salad!

A beautiful blend of bulbs: yellow onions, garlic and pickled onions. There are many varieties to choose from.

Horseradish

Armoracia rusticana

My mother's grandfather owned a fine male pig, who happened to be a horseradish addict. When the sow's grunts became monotonous, this boar would break free and dash into the garden, where he ploughed up as many horseradishes as he could find. Then he sat down and chewed on them, with tears of ecstasy flowing from his eyes. It was a strange sight, which reminded one of how little difference there is between pigs and people.

As good as gold

Of course, such creatures were not what taught the human race to appreciate this piquant root-vegetable. In mythology, horseradish was introduced by none other than the Greek god Apollo. His oracle at Delphi is thought to have said: "The radish is worth its weight in lead; the black radish, in silver—but the horseradish, in gold!" This has been doubted for linguistic reasons, but horseradish does grow wild in many parts of the eastern Balkans, and may well have been enjoyed by the old Greeks.

A root with obscure roots

All the above-mentioned plants, in fact, belong to a group with similar tastes. Its members were often confused with each other in ancient literature. This makes our research a little uncertain: for example, the claim that horseradish was known to the early Egyptians is based on a misinterpretation. Likewise, historians and botanists have placed the original homeland of horseradish in various regions—ranging from the Mediterranean to the Orient, even Siberia. Some believe that it was brought from the south to Central Europe by monks, who spread it further.

Today, the usual view is that horseradish comes from southern Russia. Together with its Russian name, *khren*, it was adopted by other Slavic nations, also resulting in the Austrian name *kren*. The Germans, who have long been notorious consumers of horseradish, found it easy to import from the East. And it plays a very German role in European cooking. Popular dishes in France make use of horseradish mainly in the province of Alsace, whose people are partly of German stock. A common French term for it is *moutarde des allemands*, meaning German mustard.

We might imagine that the standard German name, *Meerrettich*, has to do with the sea *(Meer)*. But this derives from an old Germanic word for "horse", as do our words "marshal" and "mare". The English name "horseradish" is simply a later translation. While many Scandinavians are fond of the spice, their term "pepper-root" is rather unique, and we cannot be sure whether they learned about horseradish directly

Species name:	Armoracia rusticana (or lapathifolia)
Family:	Brassicaceae (formerly Cruciferae), mustard and cabbage plants
Spicy part:	Root (and leaves as salad)
Origin:	Southern Russia, Balkans
Cultivation:	Mainly for local use in eastern and northern Europe, northern USA (especially Illinois, Pennsylvania, New Jersey and Wisconsin)
Common names:	French: raifort, moutarde des allemands German: Meerrettich, Waldrettich, Kren, Märek, Beisswurzel, Bauernsenf, Fleischkraut, Rachenputzer Italian: rafano Spanish: rabano picante Swedish: pepparrot

from Russia or through influence from the Germanic countries.

A useful cure-all

The plant's bitter root is not its only asset. In many places, the leaves have also been eaten as salad. Moreover, horseradish was once a reputable medicine, especially in the Middle Ages—already during the thirteenth century in England. It supposedly helped against fever, kidney and gall stones, hip pain, lung ailments and dropsy. In addition, it was considered to promote hair-growth, and was made into a poultice for gout. People even carried a bit of horseradish in their purses so that they would never be without money.

Since the sixteenth century, horseradish has been praised chiefly for its culinary virtues in literature. The great German botanist Tabernae-montanus thought that it whetted the appetite, and noted that his compatriots loved to eat horseradish sauce with boiled meat. In England, John Gerard's *Herball* (1597) described the plant as a spice eaten by Germans with fish as well as meat, much like mustard sauce. Another English report in 1640 shows that horseradish became popular among the countryfolk, being "best suited to those with hard manual labour, not the delicate stomachs of city-dwellers". Soon after that, it was eaten quite widely—for example with beef—in both cities and villages.

It may be worth testing the old belief that a bit of horse-radish in your purse will keep Poverty away from the door.

Best when grated

In our time, horseradish serves well-limited purposes at the dinner table. Freshly grated, it goes with roast beef, tongue, oysters, and so on. Horseradish cream enhances the taste of smoked salmon and mayonnaise. Mould is prevented by adding horseradish to preserved beets and pickles. Seamen, too, have used horseradish for protection from scurvy, as it is rich in vitamin C. On the other hand, few of us would want to gobble it in large quantities.

An edible weed

The horseradish plant, a perennial, rises to about one metre tall. Its first leaves, elongated and blunt-toothed, come from the rootstock. Then in the summer, a metre-high stalk emerges, bearing clusters of small white flowers. The fruit seeds are frequently sterile, so new plants are grown from cuttings. For the same reason, horseradish can spread itself undesirably and is difficult to eliminate. If pulled up, it will grow again from any part of the root that is left. Hence it is detested in some areas —notably the northeastern United States, where it was established by early immigrants from Europe.

The root of a horseradish planted in springtime is ready to harvest in September, but is often allowed to grow longer. Its aroma reputedly becomes sharper with cold weather. The pungent vapour, which stimulates tears, is due to an oil like that in mustard plants.

Horseradish should stay in the ground until the weather begins to turn cold.

The root of horseradish is not its only useful part. Its leaves are also enjoyable in salads.

Poppy seeds

Papaver somniferum

In classical art, the opium poppy was an attribute of the Greek goddess Demeter, called Ceres by the Romans. She was often portrayed with an opium stalk in one hand. This plant had religious significance as early as the Late Bronze Age in the eastern Mediterranean. For instance, on the island of Crete, archaeologists have dug up a statue of a goddess with poppy-seed capsules on her head, dating from about 1100 B.C. She may well have been an ancestor of Demeter, whose worship is known to have originated in that prehistoric age.

Why the opium poppy became a symbol of Demeter is puzzling. But a later myth related it to her motherly personality. By her own brother Zeus, she had given birth to a beautiful daughter named Persephone. One day, while gathering flowers with some friends, the girl was kidnapped by Hades—god of the underworld—who had actually asked Zeus for permission to do so. He brought her to his shadowy realm, where she had a lot to do, such as making sure that people's curses on each other were carried out. However, her mother went looking for her, finally reaching the city of Eleusis and becoming a central figure in its famous "mystery" rites. Demeter was so worried about Persephone during this time that she could not sleep and turned to opium for comfort.

Species name:	Papaver somniferum
Family:	Papaveraceae (poppy plants)
Spicy part:	Seeds
Origin:	Near East, Central Asia
Cultivation:	For seeds, in the Netherlands, Denmark, Germany, Greece, Bulgaria, Turkey, North Africa, India
Common names:	French: pavot
	German: Mohn
	Italian: papavero
	Spanish: adormidera
	Swedish: vallmo

An emblem of fertility

There is a further connection between Demeter and poppies. At Eleusis, she used her power to prevent the crops from growing until her daughter returned. In the end, mankind was facing starvation, which also meant that the gods would receive no more offerings. Zeus became anxious and persuaded Hades to let Persephone come up again, though only for two-thirds of every year. She had to spend the winter with her subterranean husband, but when the flowers and other plants sprouted, she could live once more with her mother.

Demeter was the European version of an old fertility goddess who existed in the Near East too, often associated with a young god—such as Astarte with Adonis in Syria, Kybele with Attis in Asia Minor, and Isis with Osiris in Egypt. The poppy may have belonged to this cult because of its own fertility. A single capsule is full of tiny seeds: more than two million of them are said to weigh only one kilogram (a fact which I have not yet checked)! It can thus reproduce in huge numbers, and was possibly thought to set a good example for the crops of farmers.

Poppies and drugs

In addition to all these relationships, we must consider the narcotic effect of opium. The high point

of the Eleusinian Mysteries was the appearance of Demeter and Persephone before their worshippers, and opium may then have served as a drug. This cannot be proved, since there was a strict vow of silence about the rite — but similar things have happened in mystery cults around the world.

At any rate, the early Greeks clearly knew the effect of the juice in the unripe seed capsules of poppies. On the Cretan statue mentioned above, the sculptor had marked the capsules with incisions of a familiar kind. Today, Oriental cultivators of opium make these cuts so that the juice will ooze out and dry into a brown, tough mass. Moreover, the plant's name in Latin *(papaver)* could be derived from a child's word *(papa)* for food, especially gruel. According to this explanation, frustrated Roman parents stirred opium into their wailing babies' suppers...

Poppy seeds are often used in peeled form, to soften their slightly harsh taste.

The use of opium as a pain-killing and stomach-calming drug was taken over by the Romans from the Greeks. However, the poppy's medicinal virtues were apparently unknown in the rest of Europe until the later Middle Ages. Subsequently, of course, the plant had a dramatic and fateful history as the source of the first narcotic to be abused in both the East and West. It also caused two of the unfairest European colonial conflicts—the Opium Wars in the mid-nineteenth century—which tried to force the vast Chinese market to buy Indian opium that the British East India Company could not sell elsewhere.

A fine bread-spice

What earns the poppy a place in this book is its value as a spice plant. The pleasant, slightly nut-like taste of its seeds was discovered

In many spice blends, poppy seeds are an important ingredient, largely because they give a thicker consistency to the resultant dish.

Cultivation of poppies is economically important in Turkey, as in several other countries—and not only because opium can be extracted from the seed capsules.

long ago. Around 100 A.D., the Greek doctor Galen recommended them for seasoning bread. That is exactly how they are used today, as well as in some curry mixtures. Their role is now rather limited, but poppy farms exist in many countries, especially in temperate areas all over the world. In Europe, the Danes and Dutch are among their main cultivators.

Finally, any worried reader should be comforted: the poppy seeds on a breakfast roll are not in the least narcotic! On the other hand, they do contain plenty of a useful oil, which is also found in various cooking oils.

Saffron

Crocus sativus

In antiquity, Crocus was said to be the name of a beautiful youth. Two different myths connected his fate with the aromatic plant from which we obtain saffron. According to one, the god Hermes loved him, but killed him by mistake—and where the boy's blood ran into the earth, the first crocus flower sprang up.

The other story related that Crocus and a nymph, Smilax, were so in love that they never separated. Yet the gods, tired of watching their courtship, ended it by changing Smilax into a yew-bush, and Crocus into (you guessed it!) a saffron crocus.

It was possibly in order to experience such passions, in view of his sexual habits, that Zeus, the king of the Greek gods, once slept on a mattress stuffed with saffron. But crocus must have been important in classical religion, since saffron was a prominent spice in ancient civilization. We would not be exaggerating to call the saffron crocus an emperor of prehistory's floral realm.

Crocus versus crocus

Saffron consists of dried stigmas from a flower in the iris family, known as genuine saffron or saffron crocus. It should not be confused with garden crocuses, such as the blue *Crocus vernalis* and the yellow *Crocus flavus gullkrokus*. Yet the latter may also contain something that tastes good—as every gardener suspects when these signs of spring are torn apart by sparrows and other winged gourmets. Saffron crocus, moreover, blossoms only towards early autumn, when each bulb gives rise to one or two purple flowers.

Where this species originated is uncertain, as it has no known wild counterparts. But it probably began on the steppes between the Aegean Sea and Iran. There is much to suggest an origin in Asia Minor, for it was long cultivated largely in Cilicia (southeastern Turkey).

Fields for the eye

Visitors in late October to Kashmir, the disputed borderland between India and Pakistan, can feast their gaze—especially around the city of Pampore, southeast of Srinagar—on the most remarkable crocus plantations, covering some 5,000 acres. These have existed for ages; saffron played a major role in old Indian medicine, centuries before the Christian era. This valley is thought to be a most charming sight during the full moon.

If Kashmir seems too far away for crocus tours, a lesser but similar experience can be had in, for example, the province of La Mancha—home to Don Quixote—southeast of Madrid. Saffron is also grown elsewhere in Spain, such as the Balearic Islands, at Zaragoza, Alicante and Valencia, and in Andalusia.

Species name:	Crocus sativus
Family:	Iridaceae, the iris plants
Spicy part:	The flower's triple stigma, and the adjacent part of the style
Origin:	Near East, possibly Asia Minor (no longer found in the wild)
Cultivation:	Spain, Austria, Italy, Greece, France, the Levant, Iran, Kashmir
Common names:	French: safran German: Safran Italian: zafferano Spanish: azafrán Swedish: saffran

Crocus sativus L.

A good deal of saffron has been produced in southern France as well. It was introduced as a crop in the county of Venaissin (now part of Vaucluse) as early as the fourteenth century. The Popes were then living nearby, and they owned the region—perhaps because they missed the saffron of Italy, from which they had been exiled. Not by chance, saffron today is associated mainly with Spanish dishes such as paella, and with southern French bouillabaisse.

The English saffron town

A dozen miles south-southeast of Cambridge lies one of the truly idyllic towns in Essex: Saffron Walden. It still reveals traces of a "golden age" when its great textile-makers brought wealth. On the town's shield are three saffron flowers, due—like its name—to the fact that saffron has been cultivated there since the fourteenth century.

This English practice, according to tradition, began with a pilgrim returning from the Holy Land. He stole some crocus bulbs in Tripolis and, hiding them in his staff, planted them at home. Their descendants not only provided spice for biscuits and bread in the bakeries of Saffron Walden, but were also used to dye cloth in the factories. But towards 1800, both the local saffron growers—termed "crokers"—and the textile industry began to die out. Even London enjoyed saffron flowers for a time, as is recalled by Saffron Street in Finsbury. Here lay large crocus fields in the seventeenth century, when Englishmen were quite fond of saffron.

Edible but expensive

Saffron crocus blooms for two weeks at most. The flowers have to be picked early in the morning, before it gets too warm. Then the day can be spent collecting the stigmas and, partly, the styles. After that, everything wilts, including the aroma. This work is generally done by women and children. They hold a

Some crocus plantations extend over thousands of acres. For almost as many years, saffron has been valued as both a spice and a medicinal plant. Such spectacular farms as this one in Spain, therefore, are not a new invention.

flower in the left hand, and squeeze off its style with the thumbnail; then the stigma is pinched with the right hand and tossed into a bowl. Obviously the process is very labour-intensive, which is one reason for the high price of saffron.

Besides, about 150,000 flowers are needed to produce one kilogram of saffron. A planted bulb takes a couple of years even to begin flowering. And once exploited for a couple of years, the plants must be dug up, cleaned and replanted. Such effort and delay make it easy to understand why saffron is the most expensive thing we can find to feast on.

The stigmas are treated a little differently in the East and West. Spaniards have a custom of drying them in sieves over low fires of coal. In Kashmir, for example, a much more complicated method exists, using a water-bath to separate the stigmas by quality.

Our oldest spice?

In the Near East, saffron has been a household word for thousands of years. Among the oldest proofs is an Egyptian medical text, written about 1500 B.C. and named Papyrus Ebers after its discoverer. It tells us that crocus (yellow, though!) was grown in the palace gardens at Luxor.

Still earlier evidence is found in Mesopotamia. The word "saffron", which we borrowed at a rather late date through Persian and Arabic, is now thought to have derived from the Sumerian language. This was spoken in the first civilization on earth, where writing also began, more than 5,000 years ago. Thus saffron may well have been used longer than any other spice plant in our kitchens.

The main value of saffron, initially, seems to have been its supposed power as a medicine—not least for the Babylonians and Assyrians. A Chinese medical book, from about 2600 B.C., contains the oldest known reference to saffron. It was claimed to give strength and stimulation, for instance when making love. Similarly, the Phoenicians spent their wedding nights on sheets coloured yellow with saffron. Their Semitic culture also created the finest love-poem of ancient times, the *Song of Solomon*, which compared the bride to a garden that did not lack saffron.

Trade with Phoenician ports such as Tyre, near the saffron fields of Cilicia, was probably what brought this "elixir of life" to Greece. Bronze Age paintings by the Minoans, over 3,500 years old, showed scenes such as crocus-gathering at the palace of Knossos in Crete. The later Greek "father of medicine", Hippocrates, wrote of saffron as a medicament. Nor did his successors give up the tradition. In Rome, around 30 A.D., the famous physician Celsus used saffron in many remedies, mainly for abdominal ailments of both men and women—but also against lethargy, cataracts(!) and poisons.

The latter application was certainly of interest to rulers in those shady days. Most famous became "Mithradates' antidote", named after a king of Pontos in northern Turkey. This tyrant was afraid of being poisoned by either the Romans or his own countrymen. To counteract as many toxins as possible, his antidote contained dozens of ingredients—including saffron—all dissolved in honey. Saffron also acquired a solid reputation in Rome against a particular poison: alcohol. Whoever wanted to stay reasonably sober at a party began by taking a dose of saffron water.

Imperial saffron orgies

Romans learned to appreciate saffron equally, however, for its ability to "shout down" unpleasant smells. Saffron water and saffron oil became a kind of environmental aid, used for example to fill theatres with a nice aroma. They were sprinkled on the seats of noble families, and even sprayed on the nobles.

A clever way to improve the odour in public places was found. The emperor Hadrian had some hollow metal statues filled with saffron water. Then tiny holes were bored into them, so that the aroma leaked out continually. Other methods were to strew saffron flowers on the floor, and to inject saffron water into fruit-baskets, as told by the author Petronius.

Hadrian also discovered—if we may believe his biographer Aelius Spartianus—perhaps the most exciting of all techniques for spreading an aroma of saffron. He let a flood of saffron water run down the steps of a theatre during a performance. And the emperor Heliogabalus, a madman who was murdered in 222 A.D., filled his private pool with crocus water and strewed crocus leaves on featherbeds where he and his guests dined.

Saffron was well known to the peoples of prehistoric Greece. This trained monkey is gathering crocus flowers in a painting from Knossos (c. 1500 B.C.).

The Renaissance of saffron

When the Roman Empire fell, saffron apparently vanished from European society. Such harmless sensations must not have suited the Germanic barbarians' taste-buds, hardened by salt and mustard. Cultivation of saffron reached Spain with the Moslems in the eighth century, and possibly spread to France; but it was primarily the Crusaders' contacts with the Arabs, from the eleventh century onward, that reintroduced the spice to Europeans. The ancient crocus was evidently unknown to them at this time, since they called the spice by its Arabic name—saffron.

Once again, the medical aspects predominated, and saffron enjoyed a fresh "boom" as an ingredient of remedies. Already expensive

during antiquity, it now became costlier due to the long trade routes from its source. No other ware was so profitable for merchants, and their guilds often adopted saffron for a name and symbol. Even the heraldic lilies of the royal Bourbon family have been interpreted as stylized saffron crocuses.

Not all is gold that glitters

The sky-high prices naturally gave rise to counterfeit saffron. This was an old problem; indeed, the Roman author Pliny considered nearly all saffron to be more or less falsified. The genuine product was mixed with yellow parts of plants such as marigold, arnica, and safflower —which took its name from that very connection with saffron. Or else the true saffron stigmas were made heavier by absorbing some oil they were laid in. Fine gypsum powder could be poured into the ground saffron, and was instantly coloured yellow by it. Much later, two South African plants were discovered (*Lyperia crocea, Tritonea aurea*) whose dried flowers look and smell rather like saffron: these are called Cape saffron.

The "cleaning" of crocus flowers—by picking out the stigma and some of the style—requires much work, and is one reason for the high price of saffron.

But the medieval market towns in Italy and southern Germany were worried about their reputations. When they noticed the swindling, they established special offices to inspect all saffron before it passed onward. In most towns, the legal punishment for falsifying saffron was to be burned or buried alive! The latter fate befell, for instance, a woman named Elsa from Prague, who helped a couple of Nuremberg merchants at this shadowy work in 1456. Eventually the authorities became more humane—or economically minded. They often preferred to confiscate the offender's wealth and spices, besides burning up the fake saffron.

A many-sided spice

Saffron, of course, is not only a spice, a perfume, and (in the past) a medicine, but also a dyestuff used widely to make colourful clothing. On Irish chieftains and Indian nabobs alike, saffron-yellow robes have been status symbols. To the Romans, this hue was the "noblest" of all except purple. Greek kings bore it as a sign of dignity, though the courtesans—queens of a kind, to be sure—got in the habit of wearing it as well. Kings of Persia wore saffron-coloured shoes symbolizing a heavenly light. In fact, the same yellow hue went beyond the realm of royal power and stood for holiness. Buddhist monks, for example in Sri Lanka, still wear their traditional saffron-tinted mantles as a mark of piety.

Crocin, the colouring substance in crocus stigmas, is so effective that one gram of it can turn a hundred litres of water plainly yellow. Thus, and with no thought of spicing, it has also been used to give a more attractive hue to some foods, such as butter and cheese.

One of the most common roles played by saffron, as both a dye and a spice, is in bread. The Romans added it to bread for fine occasions, and saffron bread has been popular in places like the Levant, England (with typical tea-biscuits) and Scandinavia. Bakers once had a custom of giving saffron buns to their steady customers at Christmas and Easter.

Saffron contains a very strong pigment that yields an unmistakable yellow colour. This has long been a symbol of status and nobility, and is still worn by Buddhist monks—as shown here in Rangoon, Burma.

A recipe with Saffron
Bouillabaisse

This fish soup from Provence was born on the shore, not in the kitchen, and composed by village fishermen rather than cooks. When they returned from fishing and pulled their boats up on land, they sorted the catch. Fine fish that could be sold were saved for the market in town. Others, too small, were popped into the big pot over an open fire. Soon the wine bottles and bread appeared, and then it was time to celebrate.

The origins of bouillabaisse emphasize that all kinds of fish go well in it. A Provençal cookbook lists forty suitable kinds, excluding only the fattest fish—which still allows us to add an eel in the pot, though perhaps not herring. In brief, there should be at least six kinds of fish, some type of crustacean, and definitely mussels. A number of the fish should have firmer flesh (eel, halibut, certain flatfish) than others (small cod, whiting). Making less than 8 servings is hardly worth the trouble.

Clean and gut the fish (their spines can be left in). Then kill the crustaceans with a jab in the neck, cleave them lengthwise and across, and crush their claw shells. Sort the mussels as usual, tapping their shells carefully and throwing away those that refuse to close; brush their backs and bellies. Next, dump the vegetables into the oil in a large pot, cover them with a layer of the firmer fish, pour in the wine, and add water to cover the fish. Season with salt, pepper and saffron.

Ingredients
(for 8 servings):

3 kg of various fish
1 fresh lobster or crab, or some scampi
40 mussels (best not canned)
3 medium-large yellow onions (or two and a leek), finely diced
2 fresh chopped fennel heads
6 tomatoes, skinned and pitted (canned ones will do)
2-4 crushed garlic cloves
2 dl (0.4 pint) olive oil
2 dl dry white wine
4 tablespoons chopped parsley
1 twig of thyme (or as much canned thyme)
2 bay leaves
1 large piece of dried orange peel
salt and white pepper
saffron
8-16 slices of French bread, and butter to fry them in

Boil with the lid on for about 8 minutes, then add the less firm fish and boil for 8 minutes more. Sieve out the fish and crustaceans, laying them on a dish; strew parsley over them and into the soup. Meanwhile, the bread slices should have been fried. Pour the soup into bowls, and put a bread slice in each. On the table should be a plate and cutlery for the fish, which the guests are to cut up and lay in their soup. One can also serve aioli (garlic mayonnaise) with this meal.

Using Saffron: Saffron can be bought in either whole or powdered form. The whole type is preferable, being at any rate more seldom falsified or diluted. One can then pull its "threads" out of the envelope according to taste and use. These should not be put directly into the dish, but laid in a little warm water until it acquires a strong yellow colour and an aroma of saffron. Then the liquid can be poured into the pot.

Herbal spices

Basil, Tarragon, Mint, Oregano, Parsley, Rosemary, Sage

By the time that traditional medicines became spices, the way was paved for their subtle aromas by changes in high-class cuisine. Salty food was a thing of the past, and people no longer needed to pour pepper on stale meat to make it appetizing. Italian, German and French cooks used raw materials whose taste did not call for disguises, but could be combined with the light touch—of unspoilt nature, garden and meadow—that goes with herbs, especially when they are fresh.

The range of herbal spices available to chefs had, however, largely been determined by their medical origins. Many of the spices to be described below have occurred in Mediterranean herbal books ever since Dioscorides, a Greek in the first century A.D., collected all contemporary knowledge of such plants in *De materia medica*. This famous work was read all over Europe for more than 1,500 years. He and his successors passed on information that was not always sensible, but it contributed to the medical practice that was developed in Christian monasteries.

Botanical borrowings

Some of the monastic orders, notably Cistercians and Franciscans, spread the ancient teachings about herbal medicines to countries outside the classical world. But in Britain and Scandinavia, for example, these plants did not necessarily exist in nature. So the monks had to keep them in special gardens, as far as the climate permitted. Thus a

(Below) Vadstena in Sweden is one of the many former Catholic monasteries in Protestant countries where wild herbs can still be found that bear witness to their cultivation of medicinal plants.
(Right) Parsley in the United States is an example of large-scale herbal spice cultivation today.

Oregano, one of the spicy mint plants.

variety of plants from southern regions was introduced to northern ones, where they occasionally went wild—an instance being the "plague root" (*Petasites hybridus*), once pathetically used against epidemics.

Most monasteries have been closed for nearly 500 years in Protestant lands, yet we can still find such foreign plants growing around them, recalling the holy communities' care for health. More widespread plants that may have the same origin are tansy, mallow, and various mints. Others have been preserved mainly in flower-gardens because of their beauty: columbine, elder, soapwort and houseleek.

What follows is only a small selection of the old medicinal plants which live on in our kitchens. To these relatively common spices, many could be added which have won favour in particular localities.

Differing tastes

Some of these herbs, in fact, have equivalents in other food cultures. Scandinavians, for instance, spice most dishes–ranging from raw salmon and boiled crabs to lamb fricassees and fresh potatoes–with chopped dill leaves. Dill is a very old spice, also popular in Russia and Turkey, though probably first enjoyed in Persia or India (where it is still grown). But it is almost unknown today in France or Italy, and is widely replaced by lovage *(Levisticum officinale)*. In the north, lovage has been rather unloved, or else it has been cultivated because of a belief that its sharp smell could repel rats and snakes.

Fireweed, or willow herb *(Chamaenerion angustifolium)*, is more widely appreciated as a summer decorative plant than as an herb or vegetable. Yet in Greenland, it is a kind of "national flower" and is used copiously to spice seal blubber.

Superstition aplenty

Folklore has not only encouraged the use of herbal spices as medicines. It also created many rules about how they should be grown and harvested in order to possess suitable powers.

The seeds and gardening were done by women, both as a practical division of labour and as an internationally recognized requirement for the products' effectiveness. In most cultures, magic and medicine tend to be connected with female work. Often, too, the work had to be done in a "queer" or "reverse" manner: the woman who sowed or harvested was supposed to use her left hand, avoid using an iron knife or looking backward while on the job, or turn her face toward the wind. Nor should the cut or plucked parts of plants fall on the ground—else they were bound to lose their power.

Both the taste and medical properties of herbs can be exploited by making tea with them. This is a glass of sage tea, which inhibits perspiration and milk production (not recommended for nursing mothers!) as well as being a mild diuretic.

Basil

Ocimum basilicum

Basil has a good reputation as an embalming herb, and was already used as such in the mummies of ancient Egypt. We also meet this tradition in the romantic poem by John Keats, inspired by Boccaccio, about Isabella—a lady who laid the head of her murdered lover in a pot of basil, which kept it fairly unspoilt. In the same doleful spirit, basil was a symbol of mourning in ancient Greece, and of hatred among the Romans.

From scorpions to sweetness

One medieval belief concerning basil was that it created scorpions. Whoever wanted to acquire such a nice pet had only to break up a few basil leaves and cover them with a pot. After awhile the pot could be lifted, and a very touchy insect discovered. Here, the medical advice in herbal books was mostly about melancholy and fantasy—if the latter can be called an ailment!—but also about ordinary sufferings, like colds and warts.

However, those of us with a happy turn of mind will think of the vigorous taste of "sweet basil". It can be added fresh to salads, tomato soup, or drinks. The dried version is suited to sauce vinaigrette, roast lamb, grilled tomatoes, boiled bouillon, liver paste, or (a specialty of basil!) turtle soup. If you enjoy basil with your coffee, be sure to choose a Chartreuse liqueur.

Harvest before it blooms

Basil began its career in India, or perhaps even farther east. It migrated to our part of the world, not as a spice in the sacks of traders, but in whole form. This is one of the few Oriental spice plants that can be cultivated in much of Europe, unless exposed directly to frost. If it is first raised indoors near a south-facing window, then planted outside when the risk of frost has passed, it will grow more than a foot tall until cut. The harvesting should be done before its buds open, since the leaves later lose the spicy quality which we want.

The flowers of basil are red-white, but not spectacular. Therefore, no great bouquets are missed by drying basil plants in bunches. They are best hung under the roof in an airy attic, though not in direct sunlight. On the other hand, neither is any harm done by letting basil continue to grow. Even in traditional countries, such as Greece, the plant is kept as a well-watered ornament, or else used in religious rites to connote fertility, and people may be puzzled to see you eating it—until they taste it themselves!

Species name:	*Ocimum basilicum*
Family:	*Labiatae, mint plants*
Spicy part:	*Fresh or dried leaves*
Origin:	*India (?)*
Cultivation:	*France, Italy, Spain, Hungary, Bulgaria, Yugoslavia, Morocco, USA (California)*
Common names:	*French: basilic*
	German: Basilikum, Königskraut
	Italian: basilico
	Spanish: albahaca
	Swedish: basil

Tarragon

Artemisia dracunculus

This spice received its name from a weird superstition recorded by Pliny, the famous Roman author and scientist. He declared that, if one carried a twig of the plant, it would protect against snakes and dragons. Thus its species came to be known as *dracunculus*, the "little dragon". A similar meaning was conveyed by Greek, Arabic and Spanish words that led to our name "tarragon"—and to the French estragon, as we also sometimes call it.

Tarragon is among the few spice plants with a probably European origin, although botanists are not sure whether it appeared first in the Mediterranean area or in southern Russia, and some even think that it came from Siberia. Its name is also unusual in resembling that of a city and province —Tarragona in Spain—but this is an accident of etymology, even if the plant grows there too!

Easy to cultivate

While never important as a medicine, tarragon soon became a popular spice in much of the Western world. Today it is an essential ingredient of *sauce béarnaise*, which tastes best if fresh leaves are used in the sauce's initial mixture. Most simply, the spice is preserved in wine-vinegar, or canned in dry form. It may, however, easily be grown in a garden corner or a balcony box, supplying aromatic leaves all year round. Then it should not be sown with seeds, but reproduced by dividing older plants in the late summer or springtime.

A snappish taste

Belonging to the same plant family as wormwood, tarragon is a perennial and reaches a fair height of up to 1.5 metres. The thin, lanceolate leaves are dense on the branches. From their folds sprout tiny clusters of flowers (glomerules) which do not look very festive, yet—in tender condition—are also quite useful as a spice, for example in a bouquet for a soup or bouillon. But be careful about the quantity: tarragon is a rather fierce "little dragon", not to be played with!

Species name:	Artemisia dracunculus
Family:	Asteraceae (Compositae), the composite plants
Spicy part:	The leaves—fresh, dried, or preserved in vinegar
Origin:	Southern Europe (?)
Cultivation:	France, Yugoslavia, Soviet Union, USA (California)
Common names:	French: estragon, herbe dragonne
	German: Estragon, Dragon, Schlangenkraut
	Italian: targone
	Spanish: estragón
	Swedish: dragon

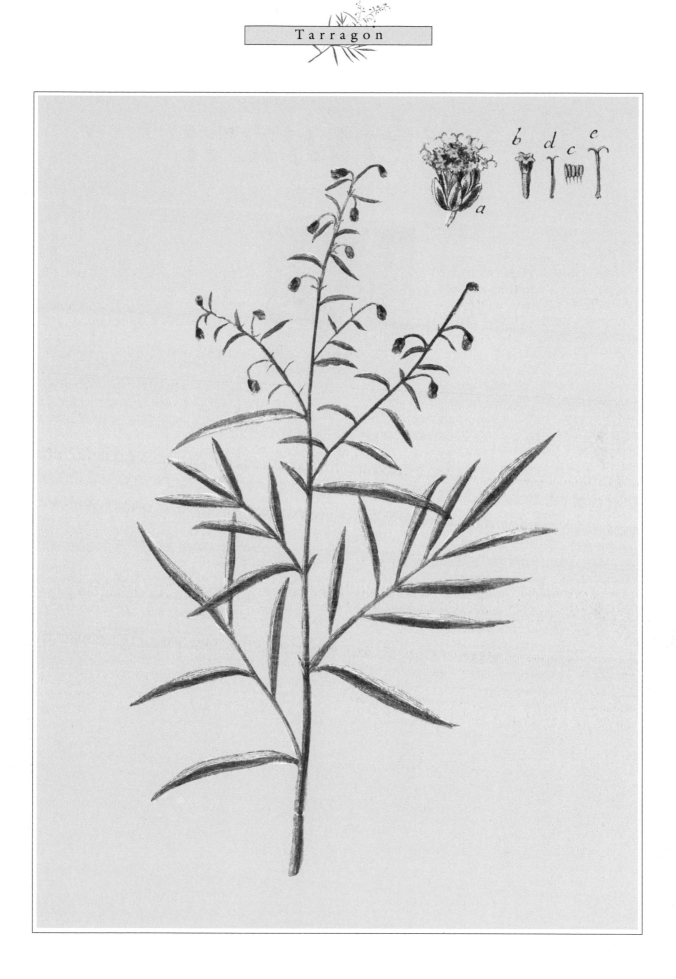

Mint

Mentha spicata

There was once a lovely nymph named Mintha, who belonged to the lower vegetation of Greek mythology. Her father was a river-god in the underworld, and she had a passionate affair with Hades, king of the dead. His jealous wife Persephone eventually surprised them in the act, and furiously threw the girl to the ground, trampling on her until she literally went to pieces. From these fragments, it was said, sprouted the herb which still bears the nymph's name in most languages, and which we continue to step on.

Flea-bait

Evidently the myth was about the low-lying kind of mint that we call pennyroyal. This spice was known in Greece already during the Late Bronze Age—according to records that were written in the palaces of the Mycenaean civilization, on clay tablets which have been discovered and deciphered during our century. Its modern species name, *Mentha pulegium*, is also partly due to the Latin word *pulex* for a lowly flea. The latter was corrupted in other languages and became, for instance, "pennyroyal".

Whatever the name, this species has been used to keep fleas away. More exactly, its aroma is supposed to attract them and then suffocate them to death. It grows wild in Mediterranean countries, and was cultivated in much of old Europe as a flea-bait. Still, it is also a time-honoured spice.

Varieties of taste

Other members of the genus *Mentha* have been more attractive for us humans. The best example is peppermint, a cross between some wild species. It can be pressed to produce "oil of peppermint", which consists mainly of menthol—a soothing substance that we can enjoy every day in our toothpaste.

As a food seasoning, mints offer plenty of local difference in taste. They are hardly used by German cooks, but a renowned sauce—made from another species, spearmint, or a variant of it called "curled mint"—is served with roast lamb in England. There and in the United States, which adopted both peppermint and spearmint at an early date in New England, peppermint is widely preferred.

Mints are generally of southern origin, but have often spread from gardens into the wild. Most species are perennial, and the long creeping stems reproduce well. Mints tend to be at most a metre tall, with pale purple flowers. The leaves are picked before the flowers bloom. Spearmint has a strong green colour, but some species are greyish, such as *Mentha longifolia* and *Mentha suaveolens*.

Species name:	Mentha piperita (peppermint), spicata (spearmint), etc.
Family:	Labiatae, the mint plants
Spicy part:	Fresh or dried leaves
Origin:	Mediterranean countries
Cultivation:	England, France, Rumania, Bulgaria, Soviet Union, Egypt, Morocco, Argentina, USA (California, Oregon, Washington, Ohio, Wisconsin, New York and Indiana)
Common names:	French: menthe poivrée, menthe verte
	German: Pfefferminze, grüne Minze
	Italian: menta peperita, menta verte
	Spanish: hierbabuena, menta verde
	Swedish: pepparmynta, grönmynta

Oregano

Origanum vulgare

Through its association with the "pizza culture", oregano has become a widely accepted name for wild marjoram. It is one of the few spice plants that originally grew also in Northern Europe—whose countries nevertheless import it from Italy, where it is much more in use.

A close relative is sweet marjoram, *Origanum majorana* (or *Majorana hortensis*), native to North Africa and southwestern Asia. This is a popular seasoning for sausage mixtures, veal and fowl.

A cosmopolite for cooks

Oregano is essential in many provincial dishes—ranging from Mediterranean meatballs to the dumplings for an English recipe called Exeter stew, and in diverse French sauces. The Swedes strew it greedily on pea soup which, often in ritual fashion, is served on Thursdays.

Both oregano and sweet marjoram are perennial shrubs, growing to half a metre tall. But in Northern Europe, the latter cannot tolerate the cold winters and is cultivated as an annual. Although prized mainly for their aroma, these plants with their small white flowers are still grown as ornamentals.

Antiseptic joy

Oregano has been known by its Latin name *origanum*, and the variant "organy", since the Middle Ages in England. These names come from Greek words meaning "mountain" and "joy". Like several other herbs in the mint family, oregano needs little water and flourishes on the dry hillsides of lands such as Greece, lending an unforgettable scent to the air even in high summer.

Herbs like oregano have also long been used as antiseptics, stomach-cures, and food preservatives. They contain "antioxidants", which can prevent spoilage of fats and oils.

Species name:	Origanum vulgare
Family:	Labiatae, mint plants
Spicy part:	Fresh or dried leaves and flowering tops
Origin:	Europe
Cultivation:	Italy, France, Spain, Greece, Soviet Union, Mexico, USA
Common names:	French: marjolaine sauvage
	German: Dost
	Italian: oregano
	Spanish: orégano
	Swedish: oregano

Origanum majorana. L.

Parsley

Petroselinum crispum

Finding a way to drink huge quantities of alcohol without becoming very intoxicated is one of mankind's oldest dreams (or rather, daydreams). The ancient Greeks had an oddly inconspicuous solution to this problem: the power of parsley. It has, certainly, little to boast about in its appearance, aroma or taste. Nonetheless, young heroes chose to wreathe their heads with parsley at parties. So, too, were the winners crowned at the Isthmian Games near Corinth—an event second only to the Olympics.

However, parsley did not play much of a role in classical cooking, either as a spice or as a vegetable. During the Middle Ages, its supposed healing qualities were emphasized. It belonged to the medicinal plants that Charlemagne ordered to be grown on his estates, and we know that it grew in the garden of the great Swiss monastery at Sankt Gallen in 820. Even so, when herbal books began to teach the real uses of such plants, not much space was devoted to parsley.

An indispensable ingredient

But on the heights of culinary culture, it won a place as early as the seventeenth century. Shortly before 1800, a French author stated that, if cooks were denied parsley, they could not exercise their art: it was simply fundamental. While he may have been going too far, parsley is indeed a standard foodstuff in our own kitchens, and few of us would want to be without it. We strew it over most of our dishes, often before considering whether some other spice might serve better.

To bring out the full taste of parsley, one should deep-fry it. In addition to the common leaf parsley, there is also a variant called Hamburg (root) parsley. This resembles a parsnip, and is a popular ingredient in a spice bouquet for making soups and sauces. It can be boiled and eaten with melted butter, somewhat like asparagus.

Back and forth to Hell

Parsley acquired its name in antiquity, the Greek *petroselinon* being a combination of the words for rock and celery. It is a biennial member of the umbelliferous plant family, and has several forms of leaves—more or less curled or lobed. All of its parts, especially the seeds, contain an essential oil (apiol) and a glycoside (apiin). The seeds take extremely long to sprout, a fact which gave rise to an old parable: once planted, they visited the devil seven times before realizing the purpose of their life! Yet they do so, and we benefit.

Species name:	Petroselinum crispum (or sativum); Hamburg parsley has the variant name tuberosum
Family:	Apiaceae (Umbelliferae), the parsley plants
Spicy part:	Leaves, or the root of Hamburg parsley
Origin:	Mediterranean countries (Sardinia?)
Cultivation:	Local in most countries
Common names:	French: persil
	German: Petersilie
	Italian: prezzemolo
	Spanish: perejil
	Swedish: persilja

Rosemary

Rosmarinus officinalis

When the Holy Family was fleeing to Egypt, the Virgin Mary is said to have once set down the Christ child for a moment in a rocky place. She noticed a little clump of white flowers, spread her mantle over it, and laid the child on this soft, temporary bed. Later, as she lifted Him and picked up her mantle, it was seen that the plant's flowers had turned blue.

Ever since then, rosemary has been a blue-flowered bush. It was still shown with this colour according to the rules of medieval art. At that time, blue—which represented eternity and heaven, truth and wisdom—was also the preferred shade for the clothing of Christ and Mary.

Ancient roots

Such tales have often tried to explain the name of this plant. But rosemary actually has nothing to do with Mary, or even with roses. It was named by Pliny, the old Roman author, who wanted to indicate that it grows so close to seashores that the foam (*ros*) from the sea (*mare*) sprays upon it.

Rosemary played a religious role among the classical peoples as well. The Greek gods of Mount Olympus supposedly valued a wreath of rosemary more highly than one of gold, and Romans beautified their house-gods with this plant, which was sacred to the goddess Aphrodite (Venus). As it was believed to strengthen the memory, early Greek students wore rosemary wreaths during examinations.

Long afterward, rosemary continued to be a symbol, mainly of fertility in the "next life" of marriage or death. Some countries still have a custom of placing a rosemary twig between the hands of a corpse; elsewhere the funeral guests lay the twigs on the grave or corpse. But in the Middle Ages and the Renaissance, rosemary was greatly prized as a medicine.

From medicine to meat

There was a delay before rosemary made its breakthrough into the kitchen. Yet in regions where meat was preserved with salt, and as early as the Middle Ages, rosemary became an important means of covering up the saltiness. It appeared more often in cookbooks from the seventeenth century onward—especially in recipes with lamb, pork or game. While most common in Italian and French dishes, it also enjoys these uses in England and the United States, being added frequently to warer for boiling potatoes and some vegetables.

Rosemary is evergreen, a labiate plant from the Mediterranean. It grows up to 1.5 metres tall and has needle–like leaves with inward–curling edges. The tiny flowers are light blue or lavender. To keep their aromatic quality, the leaves must be dried as soon as they are gathered. They retain a fresh, slightly bittersweet scent.

Species name:	Rosmarinus officinalis
Family:	Labiatae, mint plants
Spicy part:	Leaves
Origin:	Mediterranean countries
Cultivation:	France, Spain, Portugal, Yugoslavia, North Africa, USA (California)
Common names:	French: romarin German: Rosmarin Italian: ramerino Spanish: romero Swedish: rosmarin

Sage

Salvia officinalis

Here is an aromatic herb that makes no bones about its ancient medical uses. Both "sage" and *salvia* derive from the Latin word for saving, and the species name *officinalis* means that this is a healing plant. During the Middle Ages it was a celebrated remedy, and the famous Salerno School of medicine in Sicily coined an appropriate saying: *Cur moriatur homo, cui salvia crescit in horto?* ("How can anyone die who grows sage in his garden?") Skeptics might reply: *Contra vim mortis non est medicam in hortis* ("Against the power of death, no cure can be planted"). Yet believers insisted, as in the English rhyme:

> "He that would live for aye
> must eat sage in May..."

A dangerous superstition

The virtues of sage did not end there, however. It played a role in medieval magic, as shown by the following trick. Make three holes in a sage leaf, and thread them with a hair from your head, as well as one from the woman you desire; then bury the leaf under her doorstep. She will love you forever! (Of course, it could not be used to get rid of her.)

According to Jacob Tabernaemontanus, the sixteenth-century botanist, sage juice had once been drunk by Egyptian women as a fertility drug.

Today sage is a popular spice in stuffings for game, lamb and pork dishes, among others. Such recipes are richest in merry England—for example, Derbyshire cheese with sage sauce—and in Italy. Sage does have a strong taste, and one can easily lay on too much of it. Even old, dried leaves of the plant often retain a clear aroma.

A tough little treat

This "common" or "garden" sage should perhaps be called spice sage, to distinguish it from 700 species in the same family. A low bush with downy, wrinkled leaves and rather large blue-violet flowers (white and red variants also occur), it comes from the Mediterranean, and is most abundant in the mountains of Dalmatia and Macedonia. Finest in taste are the fresh leaves and shoot tips, if obtainable.

Sage can be harvested all year round, even under snow—although it is sensitive to winter cold. Outdoors, it does not grow very far north and most North Europeans have to use dried leaves.

Species name:	*Salvia officinalis*
Family:	*Labiatae, mint plants*
Spicy part:	*Fresh or dried leaves*
Origin:	*Mediterranean countries*
Cultivation:	*Southern Europe, especially Yugoslavia, Albania, Greece, Turkey; southern England, Soviet Union, USA (notably California, Washington, Oregon)*
Common names:	*French: sauge*
	German: Salbei
	Italian: salvia
	Spanish: salvia
	Swedish: salvia

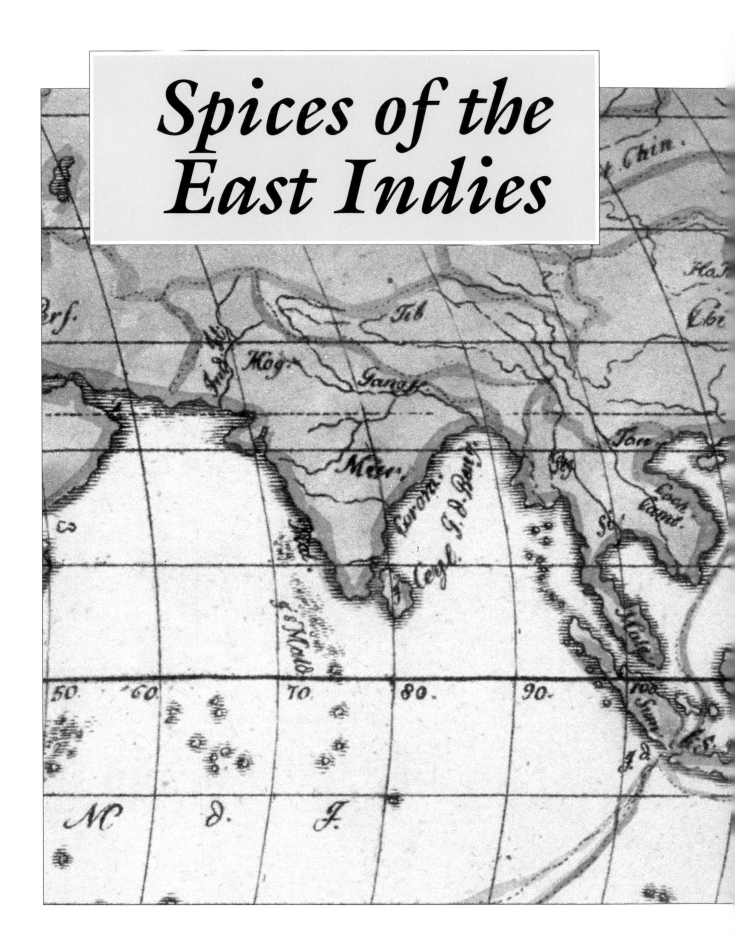

Spices of the
East Indies

The Papal Race to the Spice Islands

The Popes had two favourite countries in Europe during the late fifteenth century: Portugal and Spain. These nations had obediently supported the Church, and their monarchs allowed no heretics to stir up the orderly flocks of the faithful—in contrast to lands such as France and England, where all sorts of error were taught. But the 1490s witnessed an increasing loss of love between the two Iberian states. For they were competing to establish direct contacts with the spice islands of the East Indies.

Led by a charismatic prince, Henry the Navigator, the Portuguese had been progressing by leaps and bounds toward the southern tip of Africa. Spain lagged a little behind—she was busy throwing out the Moors—and preferred, when the time came, to send Columbus across the seas, seeking a back door to the fragrant wealth of the Moluccas. Such transoceanic trade was needed especially because the Turks had cut off the ancient routes eastward, along which the spice caravans had brought the Orient's choicest products to an ever more luxurious Renaissance Europe. Beyond the horizon awaited enormous treasures and profits.

Halving the globe

Just a year after Columbus returned from his first voyage, in 1493, Pope Alexander VI issued a bull (decree). It defined a line of demarcation from pole to pole, 100 leagues (500 kilometres) west of the Cape Verde Islands, dividing the Atlantic into two spheres of interest. Spain was to have a monopoly in the west, and Portugal in the east. The existence of other land-hungry nations, such as England and France, evidently did not

Goods are delivered, bargains struck and agreements reached, while spice-laden ships come and go in a busy port—painted by H. C. Vroom in 1640.

enter the Pope's calculations. Nevertheless, King John II of Portugal disliked the papal pen-stroke, as it cramped his sailors' freedom of movement through the Atlantic to India by way of the Cape of Good Hope.

So a meeting was called between the Spanish and Portuguese ambassadors, at the town of Tordesillas in northwestern Spain. On 7 June 1494, they agreed to shift the monopoly line 370 leagues farther west (to about 49 degrees west longitude). This eventually enabled Portugal to lay claim to Brazil—which a sailor to India named Cabral discovered in 1500 by a navigational mistake, and which even today has a language showing its connection with those colonizers.

A lucky adventure

As we all know, if an apple is split with a knife, the blade must come out the other side, too—and the same is true of the Earth. Nobody yet knew of the Pacific Ocean, or realized how large the recently found Americas were. The Indonesian spice islands seemed quite likely to lie in the Spanish hemisphere. Therefore Charles V, who was both Holy Roman Emperor and King of Spain, sent the (admittedly Portuguese) sailor Magellan on an expedition. After much suffering, he located a westward route through the South Seas to the spice islands.

Magellan himself got no further than the Philippines, killed during a foolish involvement in local politics. It was one of his captains, Del Cano, who completed the voyage. Of the five ships which had left Seville, only the "Victoria" came home—but she had 26 tons of spices in her hold. This was enough to pay all the costs and provide 500 gold ducats for the financiers to share. The fact that just 18 of the 237 crewmen had survived was of no concern to the account-keepers.

The Pope's borderline on the back of the world has made its mark on our own times. Discovered by Magellan, the Philippines stayed in Spain's possession until 1898 and are an outpost of her language and culture. The tentacles of the Portuguese, stretching round Africa, met those of their neighbour-nation in the midst of the spice islands, where Timor—as well as Macao—were the last remains of their East Indian colonial empire until 1975.

Reaping the rewards

However, neither the Iberian kingdoms nor the Vatican expected the other interested parties who soon entered the picture. Countries such as England and Holland ignored every papal ploy, and were tough and greedy. When Spain annexed Portugal in 1580, this combined empire was too huge to defend against the newcomers.

During the seventeenth century, the Dutch East India Company took over the whole of present-day Indonesia, and with it an almost total monopoly of the global spice trade for hundreds of years. With equal success, similar English companies expanded their domains and their economic power in India, dominating the rest of the sweet-smelling commerce. This situation largely endured until World War II—the beginning of the end for all European colonial rule. But by then, spice production had long since spread to additional places around the equator.

Nutmeg

Myristica fragrans

Nutmeg is not one spice, but two—and it seems to be the only spice plant which has been made a national symbol. From the flagstaffs of Grenada in the West Indies, banners of red, yellow and green, with a nutmeg emblazoned on them, flutter in the trade-winds.

For all that, the nutmeg tree comes from the Moluccas, those classic spice islands of Indonesia. The genuine article is often called Banda nutmeg, after its supposed origin near the large island named Ceram. This beautiful tree, with its ample branches, can grow up to twenty metres high. It is not only evergreen, but dioecious: the male and female flowers occur on different trees. Their oblong, egg-shaped leaves extend for ten centimetres, and are darker green on top than on their undersides. In shape they recall rhododendron leaves. The flowers are small, bell-like and light yellow—hardly spectacular, except that the whole tree emanates a noticeable aroma.

and green markings (compare the flag of Grenada!). When it ripens, the flesh bursts—this can be boiled to make good jam—and reveals its innermost secret: a peculiar crimson, lobed covering, known as an aril. The latter is what eventually fills our spice jars under the name of "mace".

Inside the aril is a core, whose hard shell encloses the shiny brown, oily, wrinkled seed—termed a nutmeg in our spice shops. The core must therefore be "shelled" in order to extract the valuable "nut". An oddity of this nut is that, after being ground up, it soon loses its taste. Hence, recipes with nutmeg often say that it is to be grated over the dish. Nutmeg and the grater are closely allied in the kitchen (as well as in the drink-bar!). To test whether a nutmeg is of good quality, one should push a darning-needle some millimetres into it. If a tiny drop of oil seeps out, the nut is fine.

Scenic fruit

A ripening nutmeg grove is a colourful treat to the eyes. The fruit resembles an apricot or large plum, and is light yellow with red

Species name:		Myristica fragrans
Family:		Myristicaceae
Spicy part:		The dried seed for nutmeg, or its dried covering (aril) for mace
Origin:		Moluccas, especially the Banda Islands
Cultivation:		Indonesia, Grenada, Saint Vincent and other Leeward Islands, Malaysia, Sri Lanka, Trinidad
Common names:	French:	noix de muscade / macis
	German:	Muskatnuss / Muskatblüte
	Italian:	moscato
	Spanish:	nuez moscada
	Swedish:	muskotnöt / muskotblomma

Sun-dried spice

After harvesting, the aril is first removed and dried in the sun for a week or two, becoming "mace" with a yellow-brown hue. Then the cores are laid to dry in the same way, until the nuts rattle inside; this takes as long as a couple of months. Later, the shells are crushed with a wooden club or in a nut-cracking machine, and are dipped in a lime solution to ward off insects. Originally the selfish Dutch had applied this

Myristica fragrans Houttuyn

Components of nutmeg: the fruit, the aril inside it (from which mace is made) and the nut itself.

treatment also to "sterilize" the nuts, so that they could not grow after being exported and risk spreading the cultivation of nutmeg to other countries.

Oil for perfume

Second-rate nuts are pressed to obtain nutmeg oil, whose users include the perfume and food industries. Like the nut, it contains a substance called myristicin, which is said to counteract stomach gases and has a narcotic effect. For want of better drugs, some addicts are even reported to "get high" on a few tablespoons of grated nutmeg—although this leaves a strong hangover, and habitual nutmeg takers have as much trouble with their heads as their stomachs.

A slow-growing tree

The nutmeg tree lives best in secluded valleys on hot, very humid tropical islands. There it may be cultivated from sea level up to about 500 metres of altitude. New plants are created from seeds, which need six weeks to sprout. When six months old, they are transplanted to a plantation and grow slowly. Only after at least seven years can the first little harvest be gathered. Most productive are trees between 15 and 30 years old. A plantation yields around six times as much nutmeg as mace: one good tree gives 5 kilograms of nutmeg, and barely one kilogram of mace.

A serious difficulty is that the male and female trees cannot be distinguished until they begin to flower. Since a single male tree is enough to fertilize ten female trees, many of the former are weeded out at the age of seven, or else suffer the fate of being grafted with female branches. The nutmeg family, too, has bisexual members.

An important trade-ware

How long nutmeg has existed in the international spice trade is a controversial question. Pliny, the Roman naturalist, wrote of a tree with two kinds of spices, but its connection

with nutmeg is uncertain. We know, however, that both nutmeg and mace were brought by Arab merchants to wealthy Constantinople in the sixth century—and that, in the twelfth, nutmeg was mentioned in various European countries all the way up to Scandinavia. It is not impossible that nutmeg was one of the new sensations for which our Crusaders acquired a taste in the Levant.

But nutmeg was not only used in food and drink. It was thought to produce a marvellous incense. In 1191 when the Holy Roman Emperor, Henry VI, was crowned in Rome, his entrance to the Eternal City was preceded by burning nutmeg, along with other aromatic spices, for several days in the streets, to lessen the typical urban stench of those times. During the rest of the Middle Ages, nutmeg belonged to the most appreciated Oriental spices. Next after pepper, it reputedly led the list of imports—and according to Chaucer, people liked to spice beer with nutmeg. Occasionally it was quite expensive: in the fourteenth century, half a kilogram of nutmeg cost as much as three sheep or a cow.

In 1512 the Portuguese reached the Molucca Islands, and found themselves in the homeland of numerous spices that were in great demand. Soon these isles were a tangle of English, Spanish, Portuguese and Dutch expeditions, fighting or collaborating with all manner of local leaders in order to control the spices which grew there in such abundance. But the Dutch prevailed, and took over the East Indies' production of nutmeg—as well as of cloves—until the Second World War.

Spice smugglers

Any country that had, within its national or colonial borders, an economically valuable plant species, which might also be cultivated in other places under similar conditions, was understandably anxious to maintain the monopoly that nature had offered it. Thus the Brazilians forbade export of caoutchouc (rubber) plants to avoid competition. The Dutch were so careful with spice plantations in their Southeast Asian possessions that they allowed not one nutmeg to be exported unless it was "sterilized" with lime or citric acid. To help prevent plants or seeds from

Fruit and aril.

being smuggled out, they banned nutmeg cultivation except on a few easily controlled isles, such as Amboina and the Banda Islands.

Problems for the Dutch were posed by pigeons which ignored the colonial laws, eating nutmeg cores and flying them to other islands. But even worse were the envious French and English. In about 1770, a Frenchman succeeded in getting some nutmeg plants to Mauritius, near Madagascar. Around 1800, France took possession of Holland and, as a result, its colonies abroad. England was then at war with France, and had no trouble in occupying East Indian spice islands. Soon, nutmeg plants were sent to the British colonies of Malacca and Ceylon, as well as to the West Indian isle of Saint Vincent in 1802. Nutmeg cultivation began on Trinidad in 1806, and on Grenada in 1843.

The Dutchmen's monopoly was thus broken—and this caused a plunge in the price of nutmeg. Holland had long tried to keep the price high, for instance by burning vast amounts of spices in its home ports and on the Moluccas. Indeed, when mace was found to be more profitable than nutmeg, a clever official in Amsterdam ordered the nutmeg planters in the spice islands to chop down their nut trees and sow more mace trees. Whether this idea was put into practice may be wondered, but it does illustrate the foolishness of bureaucrats!

Grated or whole

Today, nutmeg is not used much outside the food industry, where it flavours a variety of sausages, biscuits, strong sauces and so forth. Bartenders gladly grate a little nutmeg over certain drinks, such as planter's punch. Grated nutmeg also tastes good on creamed vegetables like spinach, and on spaghetti or mashed potatoes. In small amounts, it lends zest to stewed crabs, oysters (if one dares to stew them) and other shellfish; in addition, it

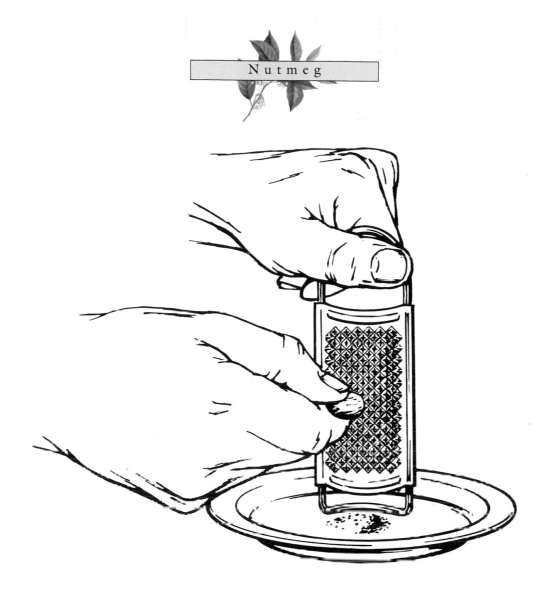

goes well with pineapple, as in mousse. A further role is played by whole mace, for example when conserving pickles and sour gherkins.

The magic of nutmeg

In the year 1619, a young man stood before the judge's bench in the Danish town of Naestved. He was accused of theft, and of something more serious: teaching a robber-colleague how to get the better of an attractive yet unwilling lady by forbidden magical means.

The trick was, first, to swallow an entire nutmeg and wait for it to emerge at the other end. Thus prepared, the nut was grated and mixed into beer or wine. Once the object of lust had drunk this love-potion, she would become like wax in the hands of her seducer, not only offering herself "to whatever he might desire" (as stated in the judgement book) but even paying cash for the service.

In this way, the young man's apprentice had acquired both love and thirty dollars from the girl of his heart—which the Court did not find very edifying.

Three centuries later, in 1917, the military hospital of Copenhagen admitted an ailing soldier. When examined, he refused to give up a little cloth bag which hung on a strap round his neck. But at last he did so, and the bag was found to contain a nutmeg. Asked why he went about with this amulet on his chest, he replied that it protected him against boils and rashes!

These incidents, from quite different times, exemplify the fact that nutmeg has maintained a reputation for possessing magical powers. Moreover, the method of seduction reported in the first case was known and practiced in Germany as recently as the beginning of our century. The two most important fields of use for nutmeg in popular superstition were, indeed, love-making and self-beautification.

A versatile medicine

Nutmeg first appeared in a Western medical context when Saint Hildegard, the "Sibyl of the Rhine", wrote down her revelations in 1147—including a whole book of healing which highly praised the pharmaceutical properties of nutmeg. Its list of virtues was long. Whoever received a nutmeg on New Year's Day and carried it in his pocket could fall as hard as he wished during the coming year without breaking the smallest bone. Nor would he suffer a stroke or be afflicted by hemorrhoids, scarlet fever, or boils in the spleen.

Likewise, if one kept a nutmeg in the left armpit when going to a dance, the risk of being snubbed or wallflowered was zero. But it only worked on Friday evenings, according to the cautious author of a black-magic book from Breslau, the source of this advice. Still, one might expect an entire weekend to be saved thereby, as long as one played one's cards right. A further charm would then be worth knowing: if one smeared nutmeg oil on a certain part of the body (essential to the present topic), the latter would remain active for several days. So, at least, insisted a monk in the sixteenth century!

Various Western authorities of the Renaissance claimed that nutmeg—taken as a medicine—prevented loss of memory, dizziness, and blood in the urine. Their Arabian colleagues emphasized the nut's value for therapy against freckles, bad breath, and itching.

Magical healing, of course, is frequently rather complicated. A good example is the following antidote for epilepsy, recommended in Slovakia and elsewhere. On a midsummer night, castrate a black cock and graft a nutmeg into him instead. The cock will have no pleasure for a year, but on Saint John's Eve you behead him, remove the nut and grind it to powder. Drinking this with some water will ward off the next attack of the ailment.

Nutmeg reveals secret powers

In the sixteenth century a famous Dutch physician, Levinus Lemnius, wrote a book entitled *Nature's Secret Powers*. Here, nutmeg played a role in an argument—typical of those days—about the characteristics of men and women. By experiment, Lemnius had established that a nutmeg carried by a man would swell up and become juicy, pretty and more fragrant; whereas if carried by a woman, it would turn wrinkled, dirty, dry, dark and ugly. The reason was obviously that men gave off healthy, agreeable vapours, while those of women were impure and tepid.

As everyone knew, the same was true of coral, Lemnius hastened to add—for such a theory gained in credibility if one could cite parallels. The professor's conclusion is not surprising: "Man stands above woman, since his nature is finer and nobler than hers. Not only do his spiritual and bodily qualities make him so strong and superior, but he has a physical energy which can even cause dead objects to sprout and grow." Nutmeg and coral, for instance!

Paté de Campagne

INGREDIENTS

1/2 kg lean calf breast
1/2 kg fresh bacon
1/4 kg calf liver
1/8 kg lard, half in thin and
half in thick slices
1 garlic clove, crushed
10 black peppercorns, finely pounded
6 juniper berries, finely pounded
1 dl (1/5 pint) dry white wine
4 tablespoons brandy
1 heaped teaspoon salt
(4 teaspoons jelly powder)
1/2 teaspoon nutmeg, freshly grated
butter (or olive oil) for the pie form

Cut the meat, and the thick lard, in cubes as small as possible. Mix them with the pepper, juniper and nutmeg. Add the wine and brandy (the jelly powder may be blended with them to make the pie easier to cut without crumbling, but it is not essential). Leave this batter in the refrigerator for some hours. Butter (or oil) the inside of the pie form carefully, and pack it with the batter—layer by layer with a wooden spoon or plastic spatula—before covering it with the thin lard slices.

Heat the oven to 180° C (356° F). Meanwhile boil a big potful of water, almost enough to fill a long oven-pan. When the oven is hot, pour the water into the long-pan; set the pie form in the water and cover it with a lid or aluminium foil. Leave it in the oven for at least an hour and a half. Uncover the form during the last quarter-hour so that the pie surface will colour a little.

Take out the pie and let it cool slowly (not in a refrigerator or freezer!). Ideally, keep it under pressure with something heavy, like a mortar otherwise it easily cracks up. Serve the pie only when it is cooled right through, suitably together with Cumberland sauce and cucumber. It can be garnished with, for example, butter-fried champignons or other mushrooms. The meal is filled out with mashed potatoes, toast, butter-fried slices of French bread, or a fresh salad with vinaigrette dressing. If the paté is sliced before serving, the slices may be laid on a serving-dish with good jellied meat both under and on top of them.

Black pepper

Piper nigrum

The idea of setting silly records in curious surroundings was certainly not invented by Guinness. Already in 1601, the butchers' guild in Königsberg (present Kaliningrad) decided to make the world's longest sausage. It turned out to be 670 metres long, and weighed about 400 kilograms—not very thick, but rather like a hot dog. This performance is, to be sure, eclipsed by the current sausage record of over 21 kilometres, set in England in 1988. Nonetheless, it can still astonish all lovers of pepper.

The guild's recipe has been preserved, and shows what an excess of spice characterized cooking in those days—one reason, indeed, for the extensiveness of the spice trade. More than ten kilograms of pepper went into the sausage batter. This is more than ten times as much, per kilo, as a well-seasoned sausage contains today. At parties in the sixteenth century, it had not been unusual for the spices to cost five times more than all the other foodstuffs together.

Not for nothing did a German troubadour sing of his joy when "the mouth tasted like an entire pharmacy". He had only to think of the beer and wine that would be needed to quench the resultant fire in his throat. The anonymous author of a fourteenth-century cookbook composed an equally bold rhyme about one of his recipes:

"With these fine spices and
    my art,
    your rump will soon begin to
    fart!"

The latter was evidently a popular diversion, even in high-class families with cookbooks. Pepper also had an early start as a means of seasoning powerful beverages, and it was used as a cough-medicine.

Pepper in ancient times

The first kind of pepper that reached the Western world is now quite unfamiliar to us. Called "long pepper", it is a member of the same genus *(Piper)* as the "true" peppers, and has a stronger taste than black or white pepper. Its two species are native to India, *Piper longum* being grown mainly there, and *Piper officinarum* mostly in Indonesia. It can be found in some pickle-like preserves.

Long pepper was originally mentioned in India's Sanskrit literature, about 3,000 years ago. The first Westerner who is known to have encountered pepper was Alexander the Great, when he marched in 326 B.C. to the Punjab in northern India. He probably tasted long pepper itself, under the local name *pipali*. This was eventually exported to the Persians, who had trouble in pronouncing the name and changed it to *pipari*. The new word soon meant a number of other kinds of pepper, too.

Species name:	*Piper nigrum*
Family:	*Piperaceae, pepper plants*
Spicy part:	*Seeds, in varying stages of ripeness*
Origin:	*India*
Cultivation:	*India, Indonesia, Ceylon, Brazil, Madagascar*
Common names:	*French: poivre*
	German: Pfeffer
	Italian: pepe
	Spanish: pimienta
	Swedish: peppar

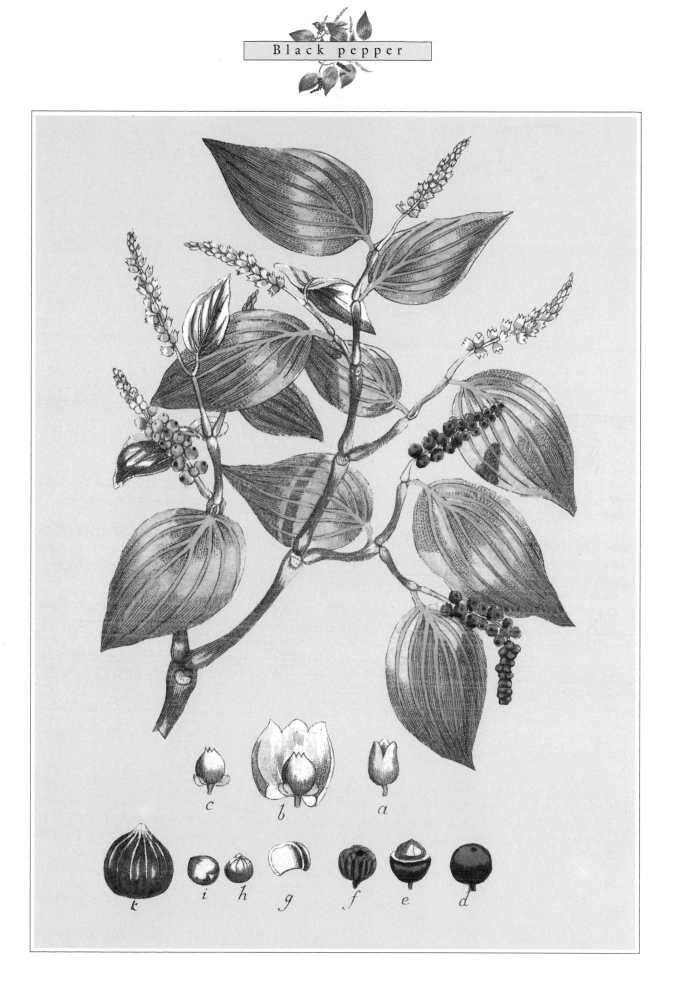

A classical success

Pepper followed the westerly trade routes to Greece, where its black form was called *pepe-ri*. But long pepper received the literal translation *peperi makron*, and was used at first only as a medicine. Next, the clever Romans learned about these species and named them, respectively, *piper* and *piper longum*. In time, the white form of pepper joined their company, being first described by Dioscorides in the first century A.D.

All three of those peppers existed then in Rome. Long pepper cost twice as much, and black pepper half as much, as white pepper. Pliny, the famous author, wondered why people wanted to eat something that tasted so bad and was neither sweet nor salty. Besides, he noted, the spice was being counterfeited—especially black pepper. Juniper berries laid in it would shrink to the same size and acquire its taste. This is our oldest example of the profitable spice-swindling racket, which later grew enormously and pursued the spice trade everywhere.

The emperor Marcus Aurelius, in 176, found that pepper had become such an important ware that it ought to pay customs duty. This was levied at Alexandria in Egypt, where the pepper was brought by Arab traders before being distributed throughout the Empire.

Thus, pepper was a much-appreciated spice even during antiquity. In 408, when Rome was besieged by Alaric, king of the Visigoths, he demanded a huge price for sparing the city: 4,000 fine garments, 2,500 kilograms of gold, 15,000 of silver, and 2,500 of pepper. His soldiers must have loved pepper—just as those from Genoa did in 1101, when they conquered Caesarea in the Levant and were rewarded with one kilogram of pepper each.

Nothing to sneeze at

Gradually the spice trade focused upon the city of Byzantium. Consumption was modest during the early Middle Ages, yet pepper can be traced in the records of monasteries, where it was probably used to a great extent as a medicine. Fresh interest in pepper was aroused by the Crusades, which—although they began with a righteous urge to reunite the holy places in Palestine with Christianity—resembled a real trade war by the fourteenth century, aiming to crush the Byzantine control over pepper and other spices.

For a long time, pepper kept the wheels of world trade turning. We still consume as much pepper as all other spices combined,

Black, white and green pepper—not different kinds, but different degrees of ripeness. All come from the same bush, Piper nigrum.

and pepper is undeniably the most versatile of them all. It was the pepper trade that primarily brought wealth to Venice and Genoa, Augsburg and Lisbon, Amsterdam and Bruges—as well as to the Arab merchants in Egypt, who made sure that the profits stayed high enough to please them.

But pepper not only became a way of making money: pepper itself became money.

During much of the Middle Ages, it served as "hard currency". Some people stored it under lock and key as a measure of their fortunes, and a man's liquidity could be judged by his pepper assets. A proper annual bribe from a merchant to a tax-collector in Venice was considered to be one pound each of pepper, cinnamon and ginger. In Germany, rich men in general were called "pepper-sacks", and—especially in Sachsen—so were poor nobles who had married rich women of lower class!

In England, a Guild of Pepperers is known to have existed by the 1150s; it joined the Guild of Grocers in 1345. Even in the early

eleventh century, ships at Billingsgate paid their toll to King Ethelred in pepper, among other things. Land-tenants commonly paid their rent in pepper, often one pound. This was about three weeks' salary for a medieval English farm-worker (in France, it could buy a slave free). Thus, too, arose the custom of handing over a single peppercorn to confirm a symbolic relationship of tenancy, which led in turn to the expression "a peppercorn rent" for an insignificant fee. In fact, when Prince Charles stepped across the River Tamar in 1973 to take possession of his Duchy of Cornwall, a pound of pepper was included in the tribute he received.

The medieval consumption of pepper grew amazingly, in particular when we recall that only the rich could afford it. Pepper spread to the peasants at a varying rate in different countries, and only in the nineteenth century did it begin to influence their cooking widely. The taste for pepper was largely due, of course, to the miserable foodstuffs in their kitchens—salted pork, more or less rotten beef (at least during the hot summer), and fish that had by no means jumped straight from the pond into the pot. These stale materials were hidden under heaps of pepper, and it was also a sign of status to serve a strongly peppered meal.

But with the rise of French cuisine during the seventeenth century, raw foods became more important than seasoning. This new fashion in kitchen culture put an end to overspicing, and pepper began to be replaced by milder spices and herbs. It was now "the poor man's spice", used by those who did not have enough money or style to eat like aristocrats. Therefore, until the advent of green pepper, well-peppered food was quite unwelcome on our tables. The price of pepper dropped so far that, in the 1840s, it was only six American cents per kilogram on the world market.

Sources of pepper

Until about 1500, it was not understood that black and white pepper come from the same plant; even today, not everyone knows this. A fourteenth-century monk named Bartholomeus wrote a book, *The Nature of Things*, explaining the connection:

"Pepper is the seed or fruit from a tree which grows on the south side of the Caucasus Mountains, in the hottest sunshine. The pepper forest is full of poisonous snakes that guard it. When the fruit is ripe, people come and set fire to the forest. The snakes flee, but the smoke and flames blacken the pepper fruits and make their taste sharper."

This miniature from the fifteenth-century Livre des Merveilles *illustrated Marco Polo's account of how pepper was harvested on the Malabar Coast of India.*

One might have asked why, in that case, some pepper was white—yet logic was not the monk's specialty. A Caucasian origin of pepper was maintained by certain experts even in the sixteenth century. This shows how long the Arabs managed to fool Westerners about the sources of their spices.

Nonetheless, green and black and white pepper are simply three stages of ripeness in the pea-sized berries of a tropical climbing bush, *Piper nigrum*. It is native to India, whose Malabar Coast (a name that actually means "Pepper Coast") supplies a great deal of the world's pepper. But it is now cultivated in many suitable places at the same latitude. A good instance is Indonesia, to which the plant was exported—probably almost 2,000 years ago. Pepper plantations were founded by the British in Malaysia as well.

A Dutch illustration, by S. de Vries in 1670, shows how pepper was harvested and tended. Black pepper is growing at left, and long pepper at right, while Capsicum *species and "Caribbean pepper" appear in the lower part of the picture. Evidently both East and West Indian varieties of pepper were then cultivated on Dutch islands in the Caribbean.*

Producing pepper

Pepper bushes need abundant rain, and a tree to cling upon. Supported today by plain stakes, they can reach three metres in height, whereas wild ones may become twice as tall. A bush is productive from age 3-4 until it is 25-30 years old, but most so at an age of around eight. The flowers, which bloom during July in India, hang in long spikes.

The berries are ready for harvesting in January of the following year, and can be picked while still green in order to make green pepper. This is either dried or canned in a marinade. Green pepper is the most recent variant (apart from rosé pepper, an intruder—see below!) and became common for cooking in the 1950s. Now well-established, it has a unique, slightly fruity sharpness that goes best with ground-meat dishes.

When the berries are faintly red (half-ripe), they can be picked for making black pepper. During pre-industrial days, they were first heaped up to ferment a little, then spread out to be sun-dried and possibly smoked. They

Like many other spices, pepper has a rather volatile (fast-fading) aroma. Connoisseurs should therefore not be content with the ready-made spice, but grind their own pepper when it is to be used.

must dry fast to prevent mildew. Drying blackens their fruit (pericarp) and wrinkles it around the seed, which is still white.

White pepper, on the other hand, results from ripe red berries. These are soaked for some days to dissolve the pericarp, so that it can be removed easily from the seeds—or white peppercorns. This was once done in tubs by trampling the berries underfoot, as with old-fashioned wine-pressing. Today, though, a lot of high-quality white pepper is made by removing the dried pericarp from black peppercorns.

Common to all of the pepper varieties is their main flavouring substance, an alkaloid called piperine. It can also be used to produce heliotropin, which is an ingredient in the perfume industry. The special aroma of pepper is due to an essential oil.

Paradise-grain

The Arabs had a monopoly on pepper before about 1500, provoking others to look for sources outside India. In 1460—the year when Europe's pioneering explorationist in Portugal, Prince Henry the Navigator, died—one of his ships returned to Lisbon, full of slaves and "grains of Paradise", found somewhere on the Guinea coast of western Africa. This cargo struck the city's spice-lovers like a bomb. Paradise-grain was an excellent substitute for pepper, and so cheap that several traders with plenty of genuine pepper went bankrupt.

The nicely named upstart was not really new. Paradise-grain had reached Europe earlier, and at greater expense, by caravan across the Sahara. It comes not from a pepper plant, but from the species *Amomum melegueta*, a member of the ginger family. Its related name "melegueta pepper" is due to the medieval kingdom of Mali, founded by the Mandingo people, who controlled much of the spice's trade northward. A tropical West African crop, it was shipped from ports around present-day Liberia and Sierra Leone. This area was long known as the "Pepper Coast"—like that in India—even though pepper did not grow there.

We first hear of Paradise-grain in 1214, at a festival in Treviso, Italy. One of the spectacles was to watch a model castle being captured by bombarding its defenders—twelve pretty girls—with flowers, candy, and *grana paradiso*. During the same century, this spice was called "Grawn Paris" in Wales. It could be bought as far north as Uppsala, Sweden, in the early 1300s. Slaves from West Africa took it to the Caribbean where, as in Ceylon, it was cultivated.

Besides its value for cooking, Paradise-

grain was used illegally to "spike" Scotch whiskey and English brandy. In England, it could help weak brewers to strengthen their beer—but King George III slapped a fine of £200 on any brewers who even owned Paradise-grain, and £500 on any pharmacist who sold it to them. Ironically, Queen Elizabeth herself had said that she liked Paradise-grain more than ordinary pepper. Today it has little importance, being used in a few pickled preserves and liqueurs.

More hot stuff

Many other pepper-like fruits grow in Western Africa. Examples are "guinea pepper" (*Xylopia aethiopica*), a member of the custard-apple family, and "Ashanti pepper" (*Piper clusii*) which belongs to the pepper plants. These spices have been valuable only during extensive interruptions—by war, for example—in the usual Oriental pepper imports. They have also been used widely to counterfeit fresh-ground pepper.

Yet a further species, cubeb (*Piper cubeba*), mainly from Indonesia, is an old spice. Europeans began to import a good deal of it in the thirteenth century. However, it had unfortunate effects on their stomachs, and became primarily a medical ingredient, especially for urinary-tract infections. A related plant, *Piper methysticum*, is used to brew "kava", a famous drink that intoxicates Polynesian belly-dancers!

The most modern variety, "rosé pepper", is not even a distant cousin of the preceding ones. It consist of berries from the little Peruvian mastic-tree (*Schinus molle*). They have a very piquant taste, and are decorative when mixed into ice cream or dessert sauce. In addition, they provide a popular condiment and are used in fish dishes.

Henry the Navigator was a pioneer of European trade around the world. He never actually took part in voyages of exploration, but did much to plan and finance them. It was thanks to him that the cheap "grains of Paradise" reached Europe.

Piles of pepper

Indonesia was once the world's leading producer of pepper, with more than 60,000 tons annually—followed by India with only a third as much. But the Indonesian plantations were destroyed in World War I, while India amplified its output to as much as 30,000 tons. Since then, Indonesia has regained a large share of the market, and pepper is also grown in other Southeast Asian lands. There is specialization in black pepper (by India, Penang in Malaysia, and Singapore) as well as in white pepper (by Indonesia). The small island of Bangka produces Muntok pepper, which is very highly esteemed.

Pepper consumption differs considerably between countries. On average per year, the Tunisians eat almost half a pound each. The amount is half as great in America, and is halved again in Europe except for Sweden. Least hungry for pepper are Chinese and Japanese, at one and three grams respectively. Its main users, however, are not cooks in the kitchen but food industries of all kinds.

In conclusion, a bit of advice. Whole pepper retains its aroma and "sting" a lot longer than ground pepper. The unground versions of black and white pepper are thus preferable for cooking.

Spices such as pepper had so high a value in former times that they were stored and transported by equally expensive methods. This portable spice-box for private use was made of brass.

Ginger

Zingiber officinale

What does the menu served in Paradise, according to the Koran, have in common with the Round Table where King Arthur's medieval knights feasted already in the present life? Very simple: the guests are treated to ginger! And this spice has indeed ranged widely in space and time. As many as 2,000 years ago, it was imported to Rome in little clay jars—much as we buy it in Chinese porcelain jars, at least when making a gift of it.

Ginger was evidently a delicacy to the ancients, if they had a healthy appetite. Nor was its appeal lessened by Dioscorides, the Graeco-Roman "surgeon general" of the emperors Claudius and Nero. In his famous book *De Materia Medica*, written about 77 A.D., he declared that ginger not only could warm and soften the stomach, but was also an excellent broad-spectrum antidote. Rulers in those days welcomed anything that helped against poison.

Candy for cave-men

As with most Oriental products, the Greeks and Romans had no idea of the true origin of ginger. They bought it from Arabian traders and swallowed the explanation: that it grew in the fabled land of the Troglodytes, who cultivated and prepared it somewhere far to the south. These odd "hole-dwellers" were a Greek name for one of the mysterious peoples living on the edges of the earth, according to ancient geographers.

Troglodytes reputedly looked ugly (today this is the species name for a chimpanzee!) and were so promiscuous that the children never knew who their father was. Most numerous in Troglodytia—a region vaguely located near the Red Sea—they were also ridiculed as "ichthyophages", or fish-eaters, a terribly low class in society. But in terms of producing ginger and preserving it in sugary syrup, they were fantastic!

The secret revealed

Now we know better. Ginger crops in that region are as fictitious as fish-eating Troglodytes. The Arabs handled ginger only as intermediaries in the stream of spices, and other goods, which came westward from countries in southern and southeastern Asia. Europeans apparently first saw ginger growing in the late thirteenth century. One of them was Marco Polo, from Venice, in China—where ginger had been mentioned by the writings of Confucius as early as 500 B.C. Another source was Giovanni de Montecorvino, a Franciscan monk and missionary, who wrote an eye-witness account of southern India in 1292.

In fact the name of ginger goes back to Sanskrit, the old Indo-European language imported to India by northerly invaders more than 3,000 years ago. They called the

Species name:	Zingiber officinale
Family:	Zingiberaceae, the ginger plants
Spicy part:	The rhizome
Origin:	Tropical Asia (not in the wild)
Cultivation:	China, Japan, Indonesia, Australia (Queensland); Sierra Leone, Nigeria; Jamaica and other West Indies islands
Common names:	French: gingembre
	German: Ingwer
	Italian: zenzero
	Spanish: jengibre
	Swedish: ingefära

tasty plant *sringa-vera*, meaning "horn-body", which must refer to its rhizome. The word was later adopted by Greeks as *zingiberis*, leading to *gingiber* in Latin and thus to various European names.

An irresistible globetrotter

Ginger was among the first Oriental spices to reach Europe. Its consumption, like the spice trade as a whole, may have declined during the early Middle Ages, but it was hardly forgotten. At the University of Salerno in Italy, the pioneering medical school taught a rule for happy life in old age: eat ginger, and you will love and be loved as in your youth! The idea that ginger was an aphrodisiac also encouraged the Portuguese to cultivate ginger in West Africa. They fed it to the men in their slave camps so that the population and profits would increase.

During the Renaissance, ginger had a high reputation in Europe. The spice dealers in many old trading cities were located on a "Ginger Street", named for their most popular ware. However, this classic of cooking was not considered fine enough for new cuisine of the seventeenth century. It remained a favourite in only some countries, such as England and the United States, where we consequently find relics like gingerbread and ginger ale.

The American revolutionaries of 1775 had ginger in their food rations. It was also prominent a few decades later when Salem, Massachusetts, became the world's biggest trading port for spices. Even during recent times in the New England states, after high-society dinners, there has been a custom of passing round a bowl of ginger jam, in order to prevent belching and flatulence.

In 1954, Sir Robert Perkins gave a speech to the House of Commons, complaining that its restaurant had not served the ginger-seasoned fowl-dish called "maupygernon" for the past 300 years. Such expressions of the Anglo-Saxon love for ginger are natural, since most of the world's ginger during those centuries has been produced in the British Empire. Nonetheless, it was a Frenchman who thought of drying ginger and grinding it into powder, which made it easier to use.

Packaging ginger in pretty little jars is nothing new—the Romans did it 2,000 years ago. These ginger jars, only a few centuries old, illustrate the wares that came to Europe with the East India trade.

The original homeland of ginger is still uncertain—it no longer grows wild—but was probably in southern or southeastern Asia, or perhaps in the islands farther east. When Europeans took over the spice trade, they hastened to cultivate ginger in other tropical colonies as well. Ginger was the first spice plant that spread in this way from the Old World to the New, particularly in Jamaica which continues to produce superb ginger. Leading importers are the United States, Great Britain, and the Arabic countries of the Middle East. Ginger in syrup, which is a candy rather than a spice, comes mostly from Hong Kong and Australia.

A subterranean delicacy

Ginger is the underground stem, or rhizome—not the root—of a tall, perennial, tropical plant. It is spread mainly by cutting the rhizome into pieces, a couple of inches

Ginger plants were shown in a book by Joan Nieuhof (1684) about a mission from the Dutch East India Company to "the great Tartar khan, now Emperor of China".

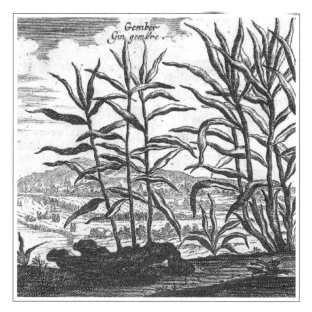

long. The plants grow for more than a year until ready for harvesting. Once dug up and cleaned, the rhizomes are sun-dried for a week, losing three-fourths of their weight.

Up to 3% of ginger's weight is a light-yellow essential oil, used in cosmetics—largely for men's *eau de cologne* and shaving lotion—and as a spice in the food industry. An oleoresinous substance, with a much stronger taste of ginger, is extracted from the ground-up spice and added to mass products like ginger ale and ginger beer.

This, of course, is a taste that we tend to reserve for sweets: soufflés, small cakes, puddings, pies and so forth. Yet the special aroma of ginger is also suitable for home-made preserves, such as sour pickled gherkins. The powder, too, is an ingredient in some curry sauces.

Finally, here is an odd job for ginger in the horse-trading business. If a generous piece is stuck into a horse's rear end, even a broken-down nag will suddenly run like a winner, and carry its tail with unusual elegance. This trick is said to lure quite a few buyers—though surely none of our enlightened readers!

(Right) Ginger originated in this type of rainforest in southeast Asia, shown here in Borneo. "Genuine" ginger no longer exists in the wild, but many of its close relatives grow here.

A complete ginger plant displays its rhizome, the underground root-bearing stem, which is cut and peeled to produce the spice.

Cardamom
Elettaria cardamomum

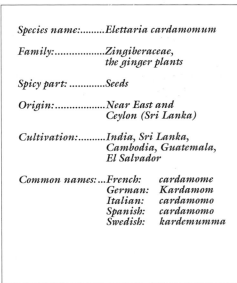

It was told of a Persian king that he had a handsome and fiery war-horse, with a single reservation. If, during a battle, the stallion's nostrils happened to catch the scent of a willing mare, it forgot its military function and ran off to fulfil its biological one. This was naturally less pleasant for its rider, and the King resolved that, to avoid such incidents in future, the stately steed should be castrated.

The grooms had led out the horse and laid it on the ground, when a window of the castle opened and the Queen's head appeared. She wondered what they were doing, and on hearing the explanation, she cried: "Why can't it drink twenty cups of coffee a day instead? The King does, and he's certainly felt the effect!"

Coffee's companion

Such stories have followed coffee all over the world. Like so many other tales, they reflect contemporary superstitions—in this case, the idea that coffee could suppress potency and libido. The same claim was gleefully made in the seventeenth century by French wine-producers, whose profits suffered from the acceptance of coffee. Fortunately, though, there were other ways of lighting a "fire", and one of the best was cardamom.

In the Near East during the sixteenth century, people began to blend their coffee with cardamom. This habit—which survives especially in Saudi Arabia—was also fashionable a hundred years later in Italy, for example, where cloves and other spices were added to the blend. The probable reason for such a peculiar marriage of aromas was that cardamom had long been famous as an aphrodisiac. It thus seemed able to eliminate the bad effects of coffee-drinking, on men as well as their women.

More than one kind

Cardamom is, however, not a very clear name. There is indeed a "genuine" cardamom—also known, for instance, as Malabar or Ceylon cardamom. But several species with similar-tasting seeds exist in the same family (Zingiberaceae, the ginger plants).

The genuine type, *Elettaria cardamomum*, grows wild in forests at altitudes of 800-1,500 metres. Its habitats are in southwestern India, mainly the Ghat Mountains of the Malabar coast (including the so-called "Cardamom Hills"), and on the island of Sri Lanka. It likes to have a uniform temperature round 22° C (72° F) and to keep its roots wet, a few metres of annual rainfall being enough! This is a tall perennial plant, its shoots reaching up to six metres, with lancet-thin blades glistening green in the sylvan shadows. Its knobby ground-trunk gives rise to flower-stems, only a metre high, and

Species name:	Elettaria cardamomum
Family:	Zingiberaceae, the ginger plants
Spicy part:	Seeds
Origin:	Near East and Ceylon (Sri Lanka)
Cultivation:	India, Sri Lanka, Cambodia, Guatemala, El Salvador
Common names:	French: cardamome
	German: Kardamom
	Italian: cardamomo
	Spanish: cardamomo
	Swedish: kardemumma

(Left) In the Cardamom Mountains of Cambodia, shown here, species of "false" cardamom are cultivated—but not the cardamom that we use as a spice, which is grown in the Cardamom Hills near the southern tip of India.

(Right) A cardamom "tree" can grow quite tall, even though it belongs to the family of ginger plants.

during much of the year they bear many greenish-white blossoms, each with a wide mauve lip in the middle. The fruit is a centimetre-long oval capsule, containing three chambers that hold up to twenty seeds. These are angular and grooved, a couple of millimetres thick, and constitute the spice itself.

Late-tamed and expensive

Until two hundred years ago, cardamom was obtained by simply collecting seeds from the wild plants. But in the early nineteenth century it began to be cultivated, at first by sowing seeds on cleared forest soil. Nowadays, pieces of the trunk are used to raise plants that are transferred to fields. Since it is a forest species, the fields must be shaded with trees.

A cardamom plantation keeps the owner busy. Flowering continues for a long time and the fruits ripen for several months. They have to be harvested when about 3/4 ripe, being plucked individually. A plant bears fruit from an age of 2-3 years (or 1-2 years later if it comes from a seed). It does so for at least 10-15 years, before giving way to a more productive descendant. The harvest depends greatly on the weather, plant disease (particularly the mosaic viruses), insect damage and so on. However, an area of one hectare should yield more than 100 kilograms of dried capsules. Under favourable conditions, this figure can be multiplied tenfold.

Once plucked, the capsules are washed, then dried for some days in the sun (becoming almost white) or for a day and night in a heated room (which leaves them greener). About 60% of their final weight consists of seeds. Certain cultivated varieties differ in capsule shape and seed size. As can be seen, cardamom plantations are work-intensive,

making the product valuable. It competes with vanilla for second place on our price-lists, behind the most costly of all spices—saffron.

The history of cardamom

In its homeland, cardamom was mentioned by the ancient Vedic texts of medicine, whose traditions went back more than 1,000 years before Christ. They considered it a fine cure for such diverse ailments as obesity and dysuria. By the fourth century B.C., it was imported to Greece, where it acquired its European name. This arose by combining the term *kard* (from cardamon, a bitter garden cress) with the Oriental word *amomon* for a simpler kind of spice.

But the later Romans were responsible for making cardamom popular and using it extensively in good cooking. They even prescribed it in medicines for prevention of stomach-aches after feasting. North of the Alps, cardamom was not recorded until the thirteenth century. It figured in herbal books during the Renaissance, chiefly as a beneficial medicine. A great German botanist, Jakob Theodor Tabernaemontanus, recommended in his book *Neuw Kreuterbuch* ("New Spice Book", 1588) that bruises be treated with ground cardamom, mixed into honey.

Since then, cardamom has spun a different story in each part of the world. No other classic spice has such a patchy geographical distribution and variety of uses. In India, it is not only a principal ingredient of curry, but also one of the spices employed to fill the betel leaves which are chewed in Southeast Asia—a common habit that does not encourage kissing, however well-spiced.

Modern markets

There are two further "cardamom regions" which, though rather small, account for almost half of the world consumption. One is the Near East, primarily Saudi Arabia. The other is Scandinavia, led by Swedes and Finns: every year they eat, respectively, 60 and 25 times as much cardamom as do Americans, Englishmen and Russians, who are content with less than half a gram per year. But while the Arabs use cardamom in coffee, these northerners tend to bake it in their bread, sausages and ground meats.

A more exclusive role is played, by both cardamom and the oil pressed from its seeds, in some candy-fillings and liqueurs. The latter are spectacularly illustrated by Danziger Gold-wasser, a spicy liqueur with a gold-leaf shimmer of tiny flakes—created in the 1560s by Ambrosien Vermöllen, a Dutch Protestant emigrant to Danzig. Many connoisseurs, too, feel that mulled wine has the correct sting only if cardamom capsules are added to the decoct. On the other hand, men coming home from a night on the town have often disguised their breath by chewing a few cardamom seeds before meeting their wives!

Well-travelled readers may wonder why we have not pointed to what may be the most exotic of all places associated with cardamom. In Cambodia and Thailand lies a range of hills, the Kravanh, which were once known as the Cardamom Mountains. This region has commercially produced "false" cardamom, mainly from the ginger plants *Amomum* and *Aframomum*. But our greatest interest,

understandably, is in the genuine spice discussed above.

Cooking with cardamom

When the Arabs and other Moslems brew coffee, it is hotter than a camel's hump at high noon—and the frequent addition of cardamom may be accompanied by a little clove, finely ground. Westerners commonly use cardamom in sweet pastries (a teaspoon is enough for a large apple pie) or buns and brioches (it is then roughly bruised). Ground cardamom can also be mixed in hamburger meat and meat-loaf (at one teaspoon per kilogram) to vary the taste pleasantly. And if you have to make sausages at home, a little bruised cardamom should be strewn in.

The flower-shoots and seed capsules of cardamom grow near the ground. It is the dried capsules that yield the tasty spice.

The size of the cinnamon quills held by this fifteenth-century merchant suggests the spice's commercial importance, as well as people's vague knowledge of the raw materials for spices.

The Romans also enjoyed a costly perfume and beauty-salve, called malabathron, made from a species of cassia (*Cinnamomum tamala*). Greek and Roman cookbooks do not mention cinnamon as a spice, but it was occasionally used to improve the taste of wine.

Perhaps the high point of cinnamon consumption in ancient times was reached by Nero, after killing his wife Poppaea Sabina with a kick in the stomach. Inspired by megalomania rather than regret, he ordered that all the cinnamon in Rome be collected—a whole year of imports—and burned on the funeral pyre.

About cinnamon in early medieval Europe, we know only, for example, that the Frankish king Chilperic II, in 716, gave a few kilograms of it to a monastery in Normandy. The ninth century brought contacts with the Saracens in Sicily, renewing the European awareness of several long-forgotten aids to cooking, such as sugar and cinnamon. This influence grew with the Crusades and the travels of Marco Polo. However, late medieval books of healing mentioned cinnamon chiefly as an ingredient of medicines for coughing, hoarseness and sore throats. Even in the fifteenth century, cinnamon was still so expensive that its importation required "hard currency", like white slave women and eunuchs. One could then read in the *Book of Nurture*, by the English author John Russell, that "Synamone is for lordes, canelle (cassia) for common people".

In the spring of 1530, Charles V came to Augsburg, Germany, visiting one of Europe's richest men: the merchant Jakob Fugger, whom he had just raised to the rank of count. The meeting may have been a bit embarrassing for the Emperor, as he always needed money and had borrowed a huge sum from Fugger. He began his call with apologies for delaying repayment, then tried to compare the warm weather in Italy—from which he had recently come—with the cold in Augsburg. Fugger opened a stove, threw in a bunch of cinnamon bark, and topped it off with the debt note. No doubt the Emperor felt warmed by this gesture, especially since the fuel itself was worth a fortune.

Cinnamon empires

It was during the fifteenth century that the Portuguese began to cross the seas for spices—not least cinnamon. Columbus sought it eagerly, though of course vainly, on the isles of the West Indies. More successful was Lorenzo da Almeida, who "discovered" the cinnamon resources of Ceylon in 1505. Previously, the cinnamon trade had provided the main wealth of the island's Singhalese rulers. Now they found the Portuguese claiming the coasts and, from 1580 onward, demanding an annual tribute of 125 tons of cinnamon.

One of them, the King of Kandy, appealed in frustration to the Dutch for help. In 1596, a few years after Portugal had temporarily lost its independence, the first Dutch naval and merchant vessels entered the Indian Ocean. Between 1632 and 1658, the Dutch pushed the Portuguese out of Ceylon. Soon the latter's cinnamon monopoly passed to the former—who dealt even more harshly with the low caste of Chalia, "cinnamon strippers". From the age of 12, every male Chalia had to deliver 28 kilograms of bark in each harvest season, and the Dutch raised this quota to an inconceivable 303 kilograms.

In return, the poor labourers got a paltry rice ration and—wonder of wonders!—a tax exemption. Many naturally preferred to escape to the freedom of the mountains, so the burden of work increased on those who remained. Moreover, execution awaited any landowner who found a cinnamon plant in his forest and did not report it instantly to the Dutch officials, as well as anyone who tried to smuggle the bark or buy it. The Dutch also learned of a leak in their monopoly: cinnamon was abundant around Cochin, the main town on the Malabar coast of India. But they bribed and threatened the local king to destroy it all, thus securing their rights.

The first plantations

Most of the cinnamon in Ceylon belonged to the King of Kandy, and he sometimes thwar-

The famous French surgeon Ambroise Paré (1510-90), in one of his pharmaceutical books (1586), found it necessary to demonstrate how cinnamon was harvested.

ted the Europeans, lowering the supply of cinnamon. In 1761, he made a triumphant raid against them, killed 7,000 Dutchmen and ruined much of the cinnamon forests, so that the spices stored in Amsterdam shot up in value. To avoid such incidents in future, the Dutch began instead to cultivate cinnamon in 1765, and great plantations arose. Yet the Chalia caste viewed this development as a danger to their meagre existence, and tried to stop it with sabotage. Reprisals followed: whoever was caught damaging the cinnamon crop had his right hand chopped off.

The plantations succeeded, and soon the King of Kandy could be ignored at his own cost. But now too much cinnamon was pouring in, so large quantities were burned and drowned in order to keep the price up. Amsterdam's cinnamon stocks also became excessive and, in June 1760, they were burned for two days at the Admiralty House. Sixteen million French livres' worth of cinnamon went up in smoke, which was said to have fragrantly covered the whole of Holland.

The struggle expands

When France conquered Holland during the Revolutionary Wars, she acquired Ceylon as well. England, her enemy, was delighted and took the chance in 1795 to seize Ceylon. The rich plantations gave birth to an English cinnamon monopoly, run by the East India Company. Cultivation was limited, so as to avoid overproduction; the jungle kingdoms were brought into the business; and the island itself was placed under the British Crown.

The defenders of the mountainous interior, though, were difficult to control. Luckily, the English managed to get hold of Kandy's prize relic, a tooth of Buddha—which made their occupation much easier, since whoever possessed it was believed to be the rightful occupant of the throne. But already in 1833, the cinnamon monopoly was doomed. For the Dutch had taken revenge by smuggling plants of Ceylonese cinnamon to Java, Sumatra and Borneo. And the French had discovered that it grew nicely in Mauritius, Réunion and Guiana. England therefore had to maintain profits

for several decades with a 200% tax on cinnamon from Ceylon. This kind is still considered to be of highest quality. However, the plantations of Sri Lanka are no longer extensive, and cinnamon now plays such a small role in the economy that it is not even on the list of the island's twenty-five most profitable crops.

Cheap at last

The colonization of Ceylon brought more cinnamon to Europe than ever before. It became so cheap that ordinary people could begin to use the spice for cooking. During the sixteenth century, cinnamon was among the most popular seasonings in the Western world—indeed too popular. Italians, for instance, poured it into most of their dishes, and the English were not far behind. At that time, a cookbook by Robert May recommended cinnamon in places that we would think strange. Great Britain is still a leading consumer of cinnamon, along with Spain and the United States.

Much cinnamon, especially Ceylonese, supplies the liqueur industry, and it occurs in nearly all exclusive liqueurs as well as various bitters. Waste products from cinnamon and cassia production are pressed to make cinnamon oil. This is widely used in cosmetics and drugs, although they have largely turned to cheaper synthetic equivalents.

Growing cinnamon and cassia

Bark from related trees of the genus *Cinnamomum* is the source of both cinnamon and cassia. The former, an evergreen, can become 15 metres tall in Sri Lanka— but on plantations it is kept as a bush, about 2.5 metres high. Its leaves are very aromatic, shiny dark green on top and lighter on below. The flowers are tiny and yellowish, bunched on the branch tips. The trees grow from sea level up to 700 metres of altitude, and need at least 100 inches of rain every year.

As long as only wild cinnamon was gathered, birds were relied upon to spread the seeds. But nowadays either seeds or cuttings are set out. When a plant is three years old, it is cut back, forming 6-8 good shoots per bush. Two years later, these are a couple of

Clove

Syzygium aromaticum

The emperors of the Han Dynasty in China, during a few centuries around the time of Christ, were aesthetes who not only enjoyed beautiful sights and sweet music. They also had noses which turned away from all but the finest aromas. As their courtiers knew little about toothbrushes, they ordered every high official—or "mandarin"—to freshen his breath by chewing on cloves before consulting with the emperor. Arriving at the palace, he would take a clove from a bowl held by a slave, and carefully suck on it.

This was the sublime role played by one of the Orient's noblest spices, when it first appeared in the pages of history. Not without reason did Dutch authors, in the seventeenth century, call clove the honey in the empire of spices. For it certainly had virtues in addition to spreading a nice smell.

Old men, cold feet

Traditional herbal books claimed that a man could regain potency by drinking sweet milk that was garnished with three grams of crushed clove. In the sixteenth century, one of Germany's most respected doctors advised anyone with cold feet to strew clove powder on his head, because it would warm him right down to the toes.

Clove trees were said to be so hot that nothing could grow under them.

Species name:	Syzygium aromaticum
Family:	Myrtaceae, myrtle plants
Spicy part:	The flowers' buds, and less importantly their stems
Origin:	Some of the Molucca Islands
Cultivation:	Moluccas, Penang (Malaysia), Zanzibar and Pemba, Tanzania, Madagascar, West Indies
Common names:	French: clou de girofle German: Gewürznelken Italian: garofano Spanish: clavo Swedish: kryddnejlika

The spice itself was imagined to be even hotter: a jug of water, left inside a clove cupboard, would evaporate in less than two days—according to a fairly serious scientific book, nearly as late as 1800. Naturally, such a plant also had to work magic against evil. Not long ago in the East Indies, natives still wore cloves stuck into their nostrils and lips, so that demons would not enter the body there.

But like many of its aromatic colleagues, clove caused trouble. Hardly any other spice, in fact, has provoked so much bloodshed and intriguing, or crime against both plants and people, as this little dried-up flower-bud. Let us trace its dramatic past through time.

A whiff of well-being

While mandarins chewed cloves in the Far East, these were being praised in India's Sanskrit literature, which called them *katuka-phalah*, "the strong-scented". This name has enabled our ingenious etymologists to explain the Arabic term *karaful*, and thus the Greek word *kary-ophyllon* for clove—which was used by Pliny, the Roman author. It is from him, at about the same date, that we first hear of cloves in the Western world; he thought that they were imported only for their aroma.

In 335, Constantine the Great sent 45 kilograms of cloves to Saint (and Pope) Sylvester I, neatly packed

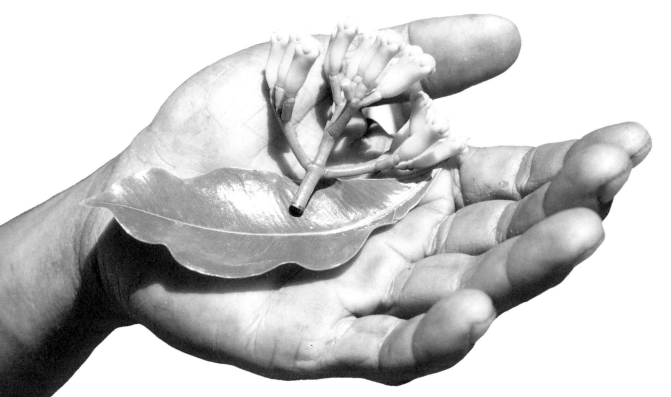

Clove buds must be laid out to dry as soon as they are picked, to avoid fermenting.

in jars. What the emperor of Byzantium meant by this gift is hard to guess—did it have to do with the odour of holiness? At any rate, a few centuries later, clove became a blessing of medicine. Alexander of Tralles—a famous physician whose works were to be read for a thousand years—maintained that clove could stimulate the appetite, prevent seasickness, and cure gout. Definitely a useful drug!

For prayers and princes

Soon, clove began to be appreciated as a flavouring in food and drink. During the ninth century, at the wealthy monastery of Sankt Gallen in Switzerland, monks sprinkled this expensive spice on their fasting-fish. In 973 an Arab traveller, Ibn Jaqub, found the burghers of Mainz seasoning their meals with it. Not far from there, during the twelfth cen-

tury, Saint Hildegard discussed clove in her book about medicinal plants. Even farther north, the spice gained early popularity, and 3/4 of a kilogram—quite a quantity at the time—was listed in the estate of Blanche, queen of Norway and Sweden, when she died in 1363.

By then, clove had long been a source of joy to spice-traders, ranging from Italians in Genoa and Venice to their Arab suppliers in Alexandria and the Levant, and beyond. Ceylonese merchants profited by clove from the Moluccas, before sending it onward to Arabia and the Red Sea. Yet the richest rewards of the European, Indian and Chinese taste for clove fell to the rulers of those small islands between the Celebes and New Guinea—the only place in the world where the fragrant tree grew. Sir Francis Drake was amazed in 1579 to see them rolling in gold; he could not have realized what the future held in store for such carefree kingdoms.

Afonso de Albuquerque (1453-1515) was one of the military men who established Portugal's monopoly over the clove trade.

A tip to Magellan

Exactly where clove grew was a secret for ages in the West. As Portuguese sailors like Vasco da Gama and Afonso de Albuquerque moved ever farther east, so did the mysterious spice's homeland. But one of the latter's captains, Francisco Serrao, reached the Moluccas in 1511 and settled on the clove island of Ternate. He became a deputy-king and died a decade later, spoiled by his native mistress. Meanwhile he had informed a relative, Ferdinand Magellan, about the local clove. The great explorer's ships brought this news around the world; and one of his officers, Antonio Pigafetta from Italy, gave the first description of a clove tree.

The Portuguese were quick to outcompete the Arab spice merchants and establish their own monopoly—using fortified trading posts, treaties with island rulers, and naval bases. Their policy was simple: all spices should be sent to Lisbon in Portuguese ships, and sold from there at a solid profit. They screwed up the prices, and executed any foreigners who traded with clove or nutmeg in the Moluccas.

But in the late sixteenth century, Portugal was conquered by Spain and her empire fell apart. The English began to prowl the same waters, as did the Dutch, who got the upper hand. Cornelis van Houtman returned in 1597 to Amsterdam with a huge cargo of spices. The next year, more than twenty ships sailed to the East Indies and came back bulging with spices.

Out of the frying pan...

The local kings, tired of being exploited by the Portuguese, welcomed both the English and Dutch. Yet it was soon clear that matters had only got worse. The Dutch proved to be most aggressive and ruthless. In 1623, they

staged the "Amboina Massacre" on the clove island of that name, torturing and killing its English merchants. One by one, they took over the old Portuguese strongpoints, while the English made similar advances in western India. Thus the original Portuguese empire was reduced to fragments—and the last of them, Macao in southern China, has little time left as a colony today.

Once Holland had triumphed in the East Indies, she needed to organize an efficient trade. Many of the spices grew only on particular islands, which made it easier to hold a monopoly over them. Clove, however, was so valuable that the complete control of both production and shipment had to be maintained, with no risk of smuggling. The Dutch allowed clove to grow on a couple of small, easily guarded islands, but laid all the other islands waste—chopping down every single clove tree and burning it.

Many battles have been fought for the sake of cloves. Shown here are Dutch ships of the seventeenth century.

...into the fire

At intervals, East India Company officials returned to the ruined plantations and checked that no new cloves had sprouted. They could not even permit seeds to be dropped there by birds coming from their spice islands. But in the case of Amboina, its size and population were too large for comfort, so they decided that it should be uninhabited. The necessary excuse was not hard to create. They installed a senile corporal and two lazy soldiers in a small fort on the island, to supervise the destruction and banning of clove trees. Just as they expected, the natives

got angry and murdered these characters. Pretending that a war had begun, the Company summoned troops. Thousands of Ambonese were killed and the rest fled, enabling the Dutch to do as they wished with the clove farms.

The same tale was repeated on isle after isle. At least 60,000 natives are estimated to have died for the sake of the spice trade. On Ceram, a still larger island, 70 ships and 6,000 soldiers arrived each year to enforce the clove ban and punish violators. Dutch farmers were brought to administer the approved plantations. But despite this, the Dutch colonists never quite managed to pacify the spice islands. In the mountainous interiors, any survivors could defend themselves more successfully and, indeed, could grow clove and find ways of smuggling it out.

Peter Pepper

Preventing anyone from taking clove seeds or plants out of the spice islands was a key element of the monopoly. Smuggling faced a death sentence—which was still applied on Zanzibar in 1972! Nonetheless, cloves were bound to go abroad eventually, and the man who first broke the Dutch monopoly was appropriately named: Pierre Poivre ("Peter Pepper"), from Lyons. Born in 1719, he began as a missionary but found business more rewarding and, among other ventures, started a bank in Vietnam.

In 1753, Poivre obtained some clove plants and tried to farm them on the Ile de France (now Mauritius). He became the island's governor in 1766 and, three years later, equipped a couple of small, fast ships.

They sneaked across to a lonely harbour on the isle of Jibby in the Moluccas, where a rajah was persuaded to sell sixty clove plants. The Dutch heard of it, but could not sail fast enough to stop their getaway. Two of the stolen trees bore fruit in 1775, and shortly afterward Poivre presented the first French-grown cloves to King Louis XVI. Cultivation spread later from Mauritius to other French colonies with a suitable climate, such as Réunion, Cayenne and Martinique.

In 1818, the Sheik of Zanzibar decreed that his realm should grow cloves, ordering the landowners to plant three clove trees for every pair of coconut-palms. Soon the whole island was a huge grove of clove. Today, though, most of the crop comes from the neighbouring isle of Pemba. It makes up 70-80% of world production, even being exported as far as Indonesia! Madagascar's turn came in 1827, and the Dutch monopoly passed into oblivion.

Clove buds ready for harvesting before they blossom.

Harvests

Cloves are the flower-buds of a tree that grows 12-15 metres high. It can live longer than a century, but is most productive at age 10-20. With time, its leaves shift in colour between yellow, pink, and dark metallic green, making it spectacularly decorative. The flowers form small bunches on branch tips, and the buds must be nipped off just when—having been green, then yellow—they turn light pink, but not yet red. This does not happen all at once in the same flower-cluster, so every tree must be harvested at least four times in a season.

The lower branches' buds, being easiest to pick, are dealt with by women and children. To reach the higher buds, men climb ladders of bamboo or raffia bast (palm-leaf fibre), which are light enough to avoid harming the delicate branches. One tree can yield up to 4-5 kilograms of dried cloves in a productive year, but otherwise perhaps only half as much. A single worker may collect up to 25 kilograms of cloves per day. The annual flowerings—and harvests—vary in number between countries, from one to three. As a harvesting period is short, supply of workers is a problem. In Zanzibar alone, as many as 40,000 pickers are needed temporarily, causing large migrations of people in Tanzania; this is also seen on Madagascar.

In the evenings after picking the buds, women and children gather in order to clean them. They are separated from their stems, an easy but time-consuming task, which generally continues on into the wee hours amid singing and story-telling.

Then the buds must immediately be laid to dry, or else they will ferment. Sun-drying gives the best results: they are spread on bast mats, preferably over a hard surface. If rain falls during the drying, their quality is worse. A thousand kilograms of the picked flowers yield 800 kilograms of buds and 200 of stems (which are also dried), and the sun reduces these to 230-250 and 70-75 kilograms respectively.

The dried bud has a tack-like shape that led the French, already in medieval times, to call it *clou de girofle*. The first term, meaning a nail, came from Latin (*clavus*), while the

second was related to the old Greek word for clove (*karyophyllon*). Thus, and rather surprisingly, the spice's English name has nothing to do with the "cloves" that we get by cleaving garlic! Its names in some other languages, such as German, also come from their words for a nail.

A spice for all seasons

Most cloves end up in well-planned meals, but a fair quantity is used for other flavouring, as in warm alcoholic drinks. Moreover, cloves are still appreciated for the fine aroma they spread. Sticking cloves into a dried orange and hanging it in your closet is a good alternative to mothballs and lavender bags. I have even seen these little scent-spikes swinging on strings over beds.

Nor is that the end of them. Betel-chewers in India consume a lot of clove for its taste. The Malays have a passion for clove-flavoured cigarettes, called *kretek*. These are also what the dried stems of clove flowers are used for. In fact, this is why Indonesia cannot satisfy the home market with its own harvest and has to import clove. In Europe and the United States, many cloves go into the food industry—especially when making spicy sauces and mixtures like ketchup—as well as into liqueurs.

From the stems is distilled "oil of cloves", whose main component is eugenol. Its uses range from perfumes and tooth anesthetics to the manufacture of another nice spice: vanillin, or synthetic vanilla. Since many people have proved to be allergic to eugenol, its

Oil of cloves was long used in dentistry as an antiseptic and local anaesthetic. This is a woodcut from a German encyclopedia of the mid-nineteenth century by Johann Weber.

role in dentistry has been disappearing, but it does illustrate how the ancient connection between spices and medicine continues until our time.

Clove is one of the spices that are eaten at very different rates in different cultures. An average Indonesian burns up about 1/3 pound of clove every year. His Indian counterpart chews only a twentieth as much with betel, although more clove is eaten in curry mixtures. And an Italian is satisfied to season pasta with just one gram of clove per year. Other Westerners, including Americans, consume about 7-8 grams annually, not only in curries but also in marinades, beverages and so on. Not a few recipes of meat and fish dishes call for an onion stuffed with cloves...

Curry powder
and its components

One of the world's first cookbooks was written in the fifth century A.D. by an Indian brahmin, Sheta Karma. He paid close attention to the priests' temple service, and their duty to prepare good food for offerings to the eternal deities. For us, who sit at mortal tables 1,500 years later, it is still exciting to note that he described a curry mixture which recalls those of recent years. Even religious texts such as the famous poem *Bhagavad Gita*, not long before the time of Christ, mentioned curries while

also warning against excessive use of them. Salt and spicy meals were thought to awaken passion and pugnacity, suiting only warriors.

Fresh is best

We should begin by reminding ourselves of an important distinction. "Curry" is not a spice but a food dish, whose name also shows its main ingredients: there are sheep curries, fish curries, shrimp curries, egg curries and so forth. Similarly, the old Tamil

The curry powder that we buy in shops is a blend of many spices. We can never grind a "real" home-made mixture as finely as this.

Curry is served at some Hindu festivals to the god Shiva, who appears at right as a cosmic dancer.

Cumin seeds being cleaned in Turkey.

word *kari*, underlying the English one, means not a spice but a sauce. A curry sauce is created by means of a curry powder, and although we often call this a curry, it should bear its full name.

Moreover, curry powder is not a spice but a blend of spices. Such blends are almost numberless, even if most of them have common qualities. Some are more popular in a given region, others elsewhere. An ambitious Indian or Pakistani housewife—except in relatively Europeanized cities—uses nothing like the ready-mixed curry powders that we buy at the corner shop or the spice store. She chooses the spices demanded by the raw materials of each meal, and pulverizes them with her spice mortar (not a grindstone!). Whether or not she adopts an electric mixer instead, the principle is the same: a curry blend should have fresh components in order to taste best.

Many Western cooks, especially if young, have learned about the charms of the world of curry from their travels or Oriental friends, and are now equipped with a rich spice cabinet where they can select the components for curry sauces, almost as successfully as their Eastern colleagues. But a basic rule, which many people in the West either don't know or don't obey, is that curry powder must be heated up, browned in a little butter or vegetable oil (ideally not margarine) in a hot pot, before it is added to a sauce or soup. A "raw" curry powder is no treat to the palate.

Once the meal is ready, pious Hindu families lay out the first portion on a plate. The master of the house carries it into the garden and places it under the sacred tree, where it will nourish the deities by way of a passing beggar or flock of birds. At some festivals, he carries a flower-strewn tray of curries to the temple and presents it to the god Shiva, who must share the gift with the priests.

Take your pick

About twenty different spices are frequently found in a curry blend. Some of them are fairly obligatory: cardamom, cinnamon, clove, coriander, cumin, ginger, nutmeg,

Flowering anise.

pepper and turmeric. Further components, depending on the desired taste, are aniseed, caraway, fennel, fenugreek, laurel, mace, mustard, poppy seeds, saffron, sesame, and Spanish pepper in a form such as cayenne. In addition, there is a special spice known as "curry leaf". This comes from a little tree in the rue family, *Murraya koenigii*, which grows just south of the Himalayas. But it plays no predominant role in most curry powders.

Several of the spices listed above are discussed in separate chapters of this book. We shall now say a bit about the others.

The preparation of a good curry begins when the materials are chosen at the shop. This is a spice and vegetable merchant in faraway Sikkim.

Anise

Pimpinella anisum

Anise is among the many examples of the aromatic qualities of umbelliferous plants with their characteristic, umbrella-like clusters of flowers. Originally a Levantine herb, it was in a perfect position to place its fruit, or seeds, at the service of the world's oldest civilizations. The Romans used aniseed as a healthful spice, for instance in after-dinner cakes to help digestion. Pliny wrote that aniseed not only improved one's breath, but made one's face look younger. If an anise plant was hung over one's bed, it would even prevent evil dreams.

In the herbal books of later centuries, aniseed was a frequent remedy, recommended for an amazing variety of ailments—and it is still used to make a calming tea. Aniseed acquired economic value as well, and belonged to the luxuries that King Edward I, in the fourteenth century, saddled with a customs tax to pay for the repair of London Bridge.

Fake licorice

The anise plant, less than a metre tall, is an annual with white flowers. Its grey-green, downy seeds are almost half a centimetre long and have five ridges (like those of caraway and cumin in the same family). While used mainly for cooking and baking, they also yield a very aromatic oil.

Often called "oil of anise", this has many applications in the confection industry, as it tastes like licorice (which comes from a different Mediterranean herb, *Glycyrrhiza glabra*)—but primarily in making famous alcoholic drinks such as French anisette, Turkish raki and South American aguardiente. For the same reason it has long been used to cover up the bad taste of medicines.

Spicy namesakes

Anise was named by the ancient Greeks, but in those days it was thought to be the same as another herb—which eventually came to be called "anet" or dill (*Anethum graveolens*), an equally well-known spice today. There is also a Southeast Asian tree, the Chinese or star anise (*Illicium verum*), whose fruit is used like aniseed.

Species name:	*Pimpinella anisum*
Family:	*Apiaceae (Umbelliferae), the parsley plants*
Spicy part:	*The split fruits (seeds)*
Origin:	*Eastern Mediterranean*
Cultivation:	*Southern Europe, North Africa, Near East, China, Pakistan, Mexico, Chile, USA*
Common names:	*French: anis, boucage*
	German: Anis, süsser Kümmel
	Italian: anice
	Spanish: anis
	Swedish: anis

Fennel

Foeniculum vulgare

The idea that fennel is beneficial to the eyes, and can even give the blind back their sight, probably would not appeal to many modern eye-doctors. Still, this is one of the oldest superstitions in medical history. It may have begun when Pliny, the Roman author and scientist, claimed that eagles became blind after moulting their plumage and ate fennel seeds in order to see again. Pliny thought that the same remedy might help weak-sighted people. It continued to be recommended by books of healing and herbal lore for 1,500 years, although it should have been disproved by experience. More plausible is the fact that English Puritans refreshed themselves during long periods in church, and freshen their breath as well, by chewing "the meetin' seed" of fennel.

Gift of the gods

The plant's name meant "little hay" in Latin, but the ancient Greeks called it *marathon*, after a famous battlefield where they had defeated the Persians in 490 B.C. They adopted fennel as a symbol of victory and success. In their mythology, a related plant which we call "giant fennel" was used by the gods to give men knowledge.

Originally an herb of southern Europe and Asia Minor, fennel was employed as a spice by both the Greeks and Egyptians—and by the Chinese—during the prehistoric Bronze Age. The Romans considered its fresh shoots to be a good vegetable. Similarly, a very juicy and mild variety, "sweet" or "Florence" fennel, is cultivated today as an annual plant in Italy and enjoys great popularity. In Scandinavia, its tasty stalks are boiled and eaten like asparagus.

Phenomenal on fish

Common fennel is a tall perennial plant, and a close relative of dill. The two are often confused with each other, while distinguishable by their aromas. Fennel seeds are oval, less than a centimetre long, becoming yellow-brown when dried. Thus they are used to spice, in particular, cooked fish—but also bread, cakes, confections, and vegetable soups. The fresh leaves, chopped finely, make an excellent seasoning or garnishing for dishes of fish, especially the fatter kinds.

Sweet fennel has a bulbous leafbase that makes a superb vegetable.

Species name:	Foeniculum vulgare
Family:	Apiaceae (Umbelliferae), the parsley plants
Spicy part:	The fruit (seeds), and the stalks as a vegetable
Origin:	Mediterranean, Levant
Cultivation:	Southern and Western Europe (notably Galicia and Provence), South Africa, China, New Zealand, East Indies, USA and temperate parts of South America
Common names:	French: fenouil German: Fenchel Italian: finocchio Spanish: hinojo Swedish: fänkål

Turmeric

Curcuma longa

Due to its intense yellow colour, turmeric is a key ingredient of curry powder. It grows perennially in the tropics, and like ginger—a relative—it has a thick rhizome with short, knobby branches. The leaves are bright green, thin and up to half a metre long, growing up from the rhizome. Among them arises a flower-bearing stalk with a leafy sheaf of yellow-white flowers.

The plant is reproduced from pieces of its rhizome, and needs about the same warm, wet climate as does ginger. At harvest time, the rhizome is dug up, cooked and cleaned, then sun-dried for a week and finally polished. The deep yellow-orange pieces are ground into a powder which is used in both food and drink, but also as a cloth dye—and in many parts of Southeast Asia, as a cosmetic for either daily life or festive occasions, such as weddings. Oriental medicine has also found it valuable.

A tricky colour

Most of India's turmeric stays in that country, only a few percent being exported. Turmeric reaches the West partly in pure form, which becomes colouring for sauces and syrups, an ingredient of some liqueurs and cheeses, and formerly also of butter and margarine. But its role in ready-made curry powder is the primary one. Turmeric is very sensitive to sunlight and should, like curry powder, be stored in darkness.

Europe got acquainted with turmeric during the Middle Ages, when it was also called "Indian (or Eastern) saffron". But it was never a leading item of trade until the fashion of eating curry arrived. Modern tourists who think they are making a "find", by buying cheap saffron in southern Spain or North Africa, often take home what turns out to be turmeric.

Species name:	Curcuma longa
Family:	Zingiberaceae, the ginger plants
Spicy part:	The rhizome
Origin:	Southern Asia
Cultivation:	India (especially the south central states), southern and eastern China, Taiwan, Philippines, Java, Haiti, Jamaica, Peru
Common names:	French: curcuma
	German: Kurkuma, Gelbwurzel
	Italian: curcuma
	Spanish: cúrcuma
	Swedish: gurkmeja

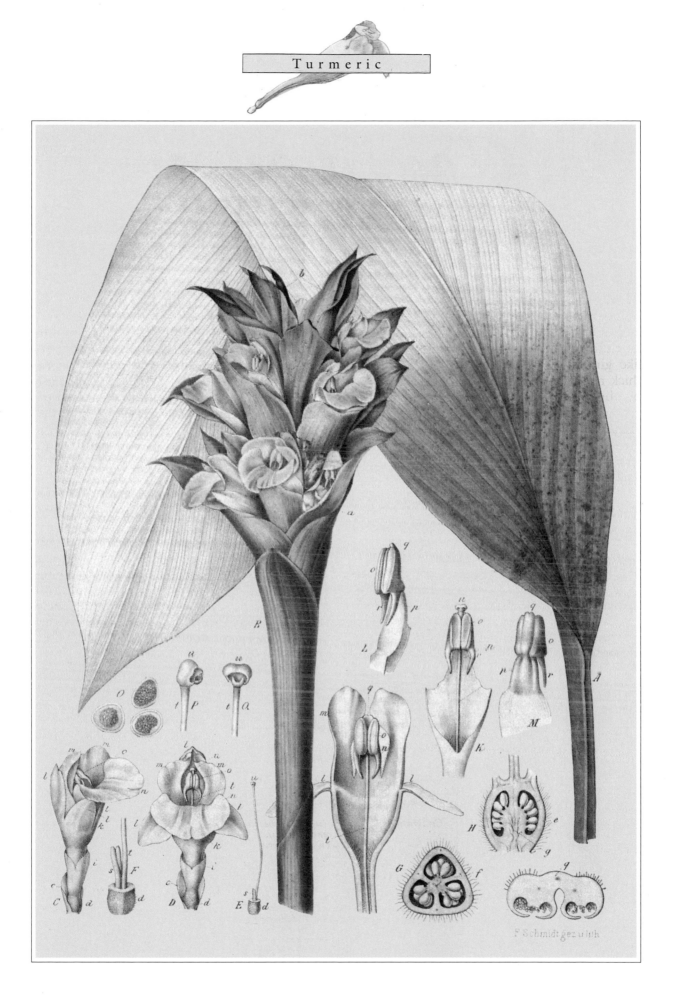

Coriander

Coriandrum sativum

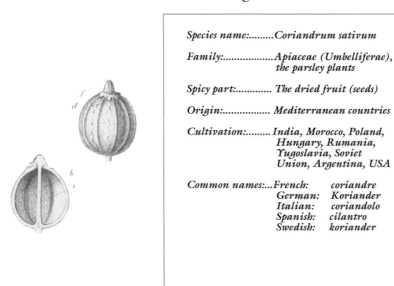

The Greeks named this herb after a bedbug (*koris*), indicating that its leaves smell rather unpleasant, although its unripe fruit has an even worse stink. Coriander has been used for thousands of years, and was even stored in the palaces of Greece during the Late Bronze Age around 1400 B.C. It was a reputable medicine at that time in Egypt, and later according to the writings of Hippocrates.

Imperially implanted

The Romans made coriander a popular spice, and spread it to Western Europe—introducing its cultivation to England, for instance. From there, it was taken to America and became one of the first spices grown in New England. But it also travelled eastward, and was among the few European plants to be appreciated at an early date in India, both as a medicine and subsequently as a spice.

Coriander is an annual herb that can grow almost one metre tall. It has finely lobated leaves (with wavy edges) and small, white or pink flowers. Its almost perfectly round fruits, or seeds, are the main source of the spice, but fresh leaves may also be used. The seeds are gathered and dried when their colour turns dark yellow-brown.

Seeds to the rescue

Coriander seeds are used largely in the production of food, alcoholic beverages, and candies. As a food spice, coriander is surprisingly unfamiliar today in some countries like Greece, but it is common in the Far East and especially in South America.

During World War II, when the confection industry had a shortage of raw materials, coriander seeds came to the rescue in a very traditional way—as "sugar drops", with a white or pink coating of sugar. Such sweets were once thrown from carnival wagons into the crowds watching them. But this was eventually thought to be wasteful, so the confection was replaced by little round bits of paper. Yet it kept its name, giving rise to the word "confetti"!

Species name:	Coriandrum sativum
Family:	Apiaceae (Umbelliferae), the parsley plants
Spicy part:	The dried fruit (seeds)
Origin:	Mediterranean countries
Cultivation:	India, Morocco, Poland, Hungary, Rumania, Yugoslavia, Soviet Union, Argentina, USA
Common names:	French: coriandre
	German: Koriander
	Italian: coriandolo
	Spanish: cilantro
	Swedish: koriander

XIII. e.

Caraway and Cumin

Carum carvi, Cuminum cyminum

These spices from the parsley family have a good deal in common, and the warm taste of their seeds has been enjoyed for ages, not least in alcoholic beverages. On both plants, the leaves are very thin and the small, bunched flowers are almost white. The yellow-brown seeds, 5-6 millimetres long, have five ridges and a crescent (caraway) or oval (cumin) shape. While cumin is an annual herb, caraway is biennial—like its relatives, the carrot and parsnip. Its fruits, when ripe every other year, are divided in half to yield the familiar seeds.

Caraway was known already to the Stone Age lake-dwellers of Switzerland. The Arabs used it as a spice and called it *karwiya*, the source of most European names for it. English cookbooks began to recommend it as early as the fourteenth century. No doubt through such channels, it has spread as far as India. We season bread, cheese, meat and vegetable dishes with caraway seeds, and drinks such as aquavit with the oil extracted from them.

A venerable spice

Cumin was mentioned by the medical authors of Egypt, and the palace scribes of Greece, more than a thousand years before Christ—as well as by the Old and New Testaments. Pliny, the Roman scientist, considered it to be a good appetizer. Interesting records of cumin were kept by medieval monasteries.

North European farmers long cultivated cumin in order to flavour bread, cheese and liquor. It is not eaten much there nowadays, but the plant still has some medicinal uses, and its oil contributes to many perfumes. Cumin seeds are popular in the cuisine of the Third World, and their greatest demand is for making curry and chili powders. In the USA, cumin consumption has multiplied forty-fold during our century. Western food industries also add cumin to cured meats and chutneys.

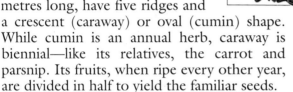

Species name:.........Carum carvi	Species name:..........Cuminum cyminum
Family:................. Apiaceae (Umbelliferae), the parsley plants	Family:....................Apiaceae (Umbelliferae), the parsley plants
Spicy part:............. The fruit (seeds)	Spicy part:...............The fruit (seeds)
Origin:.................. Europe, western Asia, North Africa	Origin:....................East Mediterranean, Near East
Cultivation:......... Europe, especially the Netherlands, Germany, Scandinavia, Hungary, Rumania, Czechoslovakia, Italy, Spain; Turkey	Cultivation:............Iran, Turkey, India, China, Indonesia, Japan, southern Soviet Union, Morocco, Mexico
Common names:... French: carvi German: Kümmel Italian: carvi Spanish: alcaravea Swedish: kummin	Common names:.....French: cumin German: Kreuzkümmel Italian: comino Spanish: comino Swedish: spiskummin

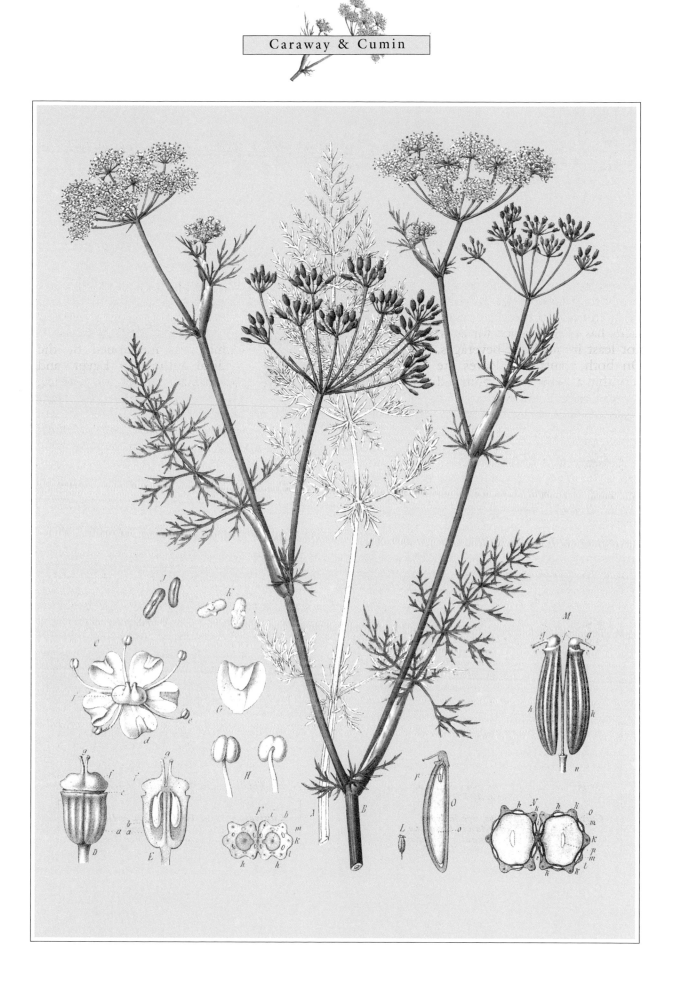

Sesame

Sesamum indicum

Sesame is a metre-high plant that originally grew in Indonesia and East Africa, but was spread in early times to other parts of Asia and to North Africa. Probably the world's oldest oil plant, it was cultivated in Mesopotamia as long ago as 1600 B.C. Its seeds contain considerable amounts—almost half their volume—of an oil that was, and still is, good for cooking. Before the time of Christ, sesame was exported from India through the Red Sea to Europe. Later, great quantities were produced in Egypt and shipped, for instance, to Italian ports. West African slaves took the seeds to America, where they grew sesame and called it "benne"—a name that can still be heard in South America.

A useful oil

The plant has beautiful flowers similar to those of foxglove. They yield small, flat, oval seeds, about 3 mm long and 1 mm thick. In whole form, these are mainly strewn on bread—giving it a faintly nutty taste after baking. (You may well find this in the next hamburger bun you buy!) But the leading role of sesame, at present, is as a source of oil. Rich in polyunsaturated fatty acids, the oil has served increasingly to manufacture margarine, cooking oils, dressings and so on.

As a result, the cultivation of sesame has grown enormously, not least in America (for example in Texas, Louisiana, California and Arizona). In China, the biggest producer, sesame seeds are used not only to extract oil, but also in several traditional kinds of candy and cake. Moreover, as in India, the Chinese burn sesame oil in lamps.

Forgettably familiar

What does the famous command "Open, Sesame!" have to do with the spice? Ali Baba, the poor hero in *The Thousand and One Nights*, learned by chance that this magic formula opened the cave where the Forty Thieves hid their treasure. His wicked brother wanted to repeat the trick, but could not remember the word "sesame" and tried other names of crops—all in vain. The joke was that "sesame" could easily be forgotten because it was an everyday term. It certainly shows how well-known the spice was to the Arabs a thousand years ago.

Species name:	*Sesamum indicum<*
Family:	*Pedaliaceae, sesame plants*
Spicy part:	*Seeds*
Origin:	*Tropical Asia and Africa*
Cultivation:	*India, China, Sudan, Mexico, USA*
Common names:	*French: sésame*
	German: Sesam
	Italian: sesamo
	Spanish: ajonjolí
	Swedish: sesam

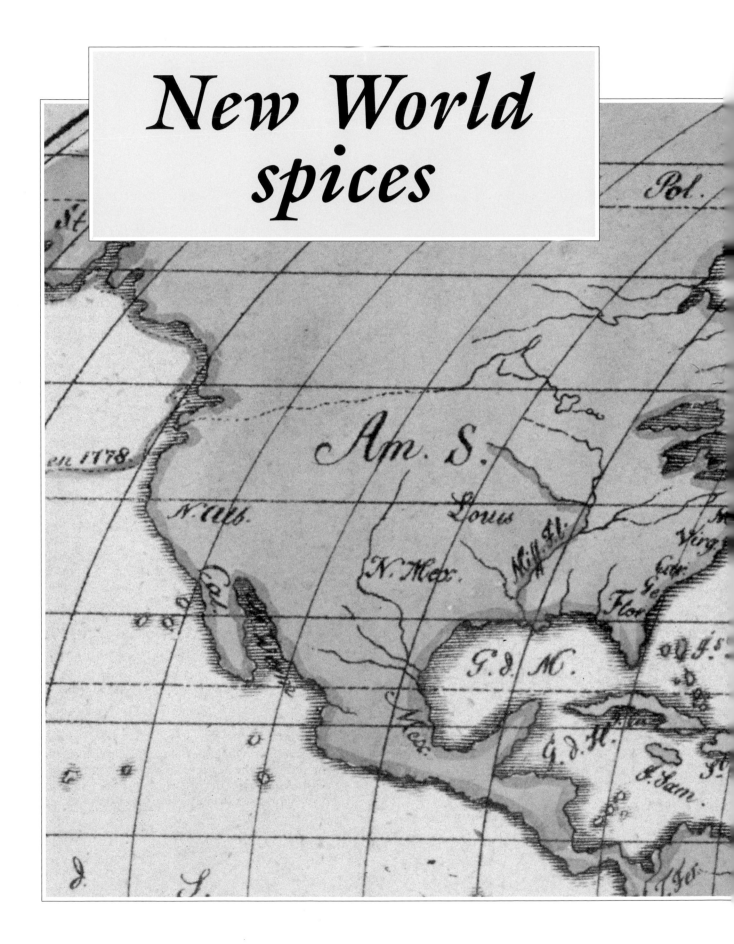

New World spices

Worlds in collision

It is 500 years since Europeans discovered America. This fateful event in world history was, as we know, not the slightest cause for joy among native Americans of that time. Only a few decades were needed for fortune-hunters and marauders from the Old World to overthrow civilizations, pillage whatever they could, and ship home as much booty as possible.

But the gold ran out and the easily won kingdoms, like their rulers, are long gone and nearly forgotten. What the sixteenth-century *conquistadores* did not guess was that, during the coming centuries, Europe was to be enriched far more than by gold and silver, thanks to a steady stream of other innovations from the New World—relatively ordinary things which, as a whole, would have greater significance for Europeans and their style of life than all the ornaments of the Aztecs and Incas.

Separate destinies

America was populated, during a period of ice in the early Stone Age, by Mongolian folk who wandered from Asia over the Bering Strait, which was then dry land. These people spread across the gigantic continent and established themselves as hunters of the abundant wild game on prairies and in virgin forests. But when the last Ice Age glaciers melted and the sea level rose, the connection with Asia was cut off, and cultures in the New World developed independently of those in the Old.

Progress was basically similar in both regions: the hunters became farmers and began to keep cattle. However, the natural environments were very different, so that distinctive animals and plants were bred and cultivated.

(**Above**) *An exchange of gifts between Indians in Florida and European explorers, according to an early German engraving by Theodor de Bry.*

(**Left**) *The ship "Santa Maria" in which Columbus reached the New World on October 12, 1492, opening a new chapter in the history of spices as well. This was a Dutch painting by A. van Eertvelt (1590-1652).*

Whereas the inhabitants of Eurasia had cows and sheep, ducks and chickens, American Indians kept llamas and turkeys. Rice and corn, rye and wheat were grown in the Old World, yet maize was cultivated in the New. In the Eastern Hemisphere people drank wine and beer, while in the Western they got dizzy by chewing coca leaves and cactus. Coffee was adopted by the Arabs and tea by the Chinese, but chocolate by the Indians.

Green outlasts gold

When the initial lust for wealth in the Americas had died down, Europeans turned to other customs of the newly discovered tribes and started to imitate these. The quick-est loan to cross the Atlantic was hardly a positive one—syphilis. Only a few years after Columbus returned, this disease spread like a plague across Europe, until then happily promiscuous. In exchange, Europeans brought measles to America, and it killed the natives like flies.

But gradually one New World benefit after another became known in the Old World, and often with greater appreciation than in its homeland. People were soon smoking tobacco, eating tomatoes, harvesting potatoes, and sipping chocolate to an extent that surpassed the Indians. And their imports of Oriental spices were matched by those from the Americas: allspice, chili, paprika, pimiento, and mild vanilla...

Vanilla

Vanilla planifolia

On September 14, 1502, a European tasted vanilla on his tongue for the first time. It happened in Nicaragua, and the tongue belonged to Christopher Columbus, making his fourth and final voyage in search of a route to India. The vanilla was in a cup of chocolate that he drank together with a local chieftain, who thereby honored the strange guest very highly, since this drink was normally reserved for princes and their equals. During the hesitant conversation over cups of chocolate, Columbus also heard something which led him to write home to his King, saying that he now had just twelve days' sail to reach Japan...

An exotic beverage

Among the Aztecs, chocolate was not only a drink. The beans of the cacao plant functioned as coinage in Montezuma's realm. As soon as Cortez had conquered its capital city, he rushed to the royal treasure chamber, hoping to find a heap of gold. The treasure turned out to be a pile of cacao beans! Still, on the local market in the year 1513, you could buy a fine slave or wife for 100 of these beans, and a night with one of the city's best cour-

A cacao fruit (pod) with its beans (seeds) exposed.

Species name:.........	*Vanilla planifolia*
Family:.................	*Orchidaceae, the orchid plants*
Spicy part:..............	*The cured, dried fruits*
Origin:..................	*Central America, West Indies, northern South America*
Cultivation:..........	*Madagascar, Comoro Islands, Reunion, French Polynesia, Tahiti, Indonesia, Malaysia, Mozambique, Seychelles, Uganda, Guatemala, Mexico*
Common names:....	*French: vanille* *German: Vanille* *Italian: vaniglia* *Spanish: vainilla* *Swedish: vanilj*

tesans for only two beans—so the find was not entirely worthless.

At that time, an officer of Cortez named Bernal Diaz was already acquainted with the drink in question. Montezuma had served him chocolate in a golden cup with a golden spoon, which he admired more than its tasty contents. Aztec chocolate was a savoury mess, flavoured with—among other things—vanilla, red pepper, maize flour, and sometimes honey. The mixture was thickened with a red plant juice which made one think that one was about to drink blood.

Markets for vanilla

Why so much talk about chocolate instead of vanilla? The purpose of vanilla in ancient Mexico, and for quite a while even in old Europe, was to improve the taste of chocolate. This is still its main role, besides helping to flavour ice creams around the world. Therefore vanilla tended to travel along with chocolate. Called *tlilxochitl* by the Aztecs, vanilla was harvested, fermented and dried by the Indians of Central America in order to be crushed and mixed with chocolate powder.

The Spaniards took the new drink home, where it became very popular, and they have since been the world's largest consumers of chocolate. In addition to chocolate, vanilla was imported from Mexico,

Vanilla planifolia Andrews.

and the two products spread together from Spain throughout all of Europe. Thus, for example, the spice's name in European languages is always an adaptation of the Spanish *vainilla*. This in turn is a diminutive of the Spanish form of Latin *vagina*, and refers to the sheath-like form of the vanilla seed-capsule.

It was in 1602 that Hugh Morgan, the English pharmacist at the court of Queen Elizabeth I, proudly discovered that vanilla could be used all by itself as a pleasant sweetener in candies. During the eighteenth century, sophisticated Frenchmen even introduced a custom of spicing their tobacco with vanilla. But perhaps what came to mean most for the growing European interest in vanilla was an announcement by one of that century's better-known physicians, a German named Bezaar Zimmermann: vanilla was an outstanding aphrodisiac! In his article "On experiences" (1762), he claimed that no fewer than 342 impotent men, by drinking vanilla decoctions, had been changed into astonishing lovers of at least as many women. Other doctors found that vanilla could cure stomach ulcers, stimulate dullards, and stop all sorts of poisons. Until 1910 it was included in the *United States Pharmacopoeia*. Today, without doubt, such uses have been forgotten, and there are probably not many people who eat vanilla ice cream to improve their performance in bed.

Columbus was presumably the first European to taste chocolate and vanilla, but he could not have guessed how valuable they would become to the world.

A large, lazy family

Of all plant families, the orchids include the most species — over 20,000. Yet strictly speaking, they are useless, except for the effect which orchid bouquets can have on beautiful women (who, however, normally do not eat them up). The only one of those 20,000 species to earn some practical role in daily life has been, in fact, vanilla.

About fifty species make up the genus *Vanilla*, but only *Vanilla planifolia* (or *fragrans*, as it was once called) produces genuine vanilla. A couple of other species are cultivated for manufacture of a rather useful, though less aromatic, variant of vanilla. They are *Vanilla pampona* and *Vanilla tahitiensis*, both containing only a third as much of the substance "vanillin" as does the genuine kind. This is the chemical compound which gives vanilla plants their particular aroma and taste. The amount of vanillin in the plant seeds is very small, only 2-3% of their weight. No less tantalizing is the sound of vanillin's scientific name: 4-hydroxy-3-methoxy-benzaldehyde!

In the wild, a vanilla plant is a lush trailing herb. It climbs 25-30 metres (80-100 feet) in its proper environment, the tropical rain forest, where tall trees enable it to reach up

(Left) Vanilla was originally used by Central American peoples to spice chocolate, whose source—cacao—had great economic importance. Shown here is a Maya god related to cacao.

(Right) Vanilla pods at harvest time look rather like string beans. The vanilla plants need careful tending, but the pods are even more delicate once they are picked.

to the sunlight, holding onto them by sending out numerous rope-like aerial roots. Its stem is fleshy and succulent; the blades—up to 25 cm (10 inches) long—are smooth, shiny, thick, flat, and oblong-lanceolate. The flowers are certainly rather large at 5-7 cm (2-3 in) and smell fine; but their yellow-white appearance is not so impressive, and they definitely belong to the Cinderellas of the orchid family. They form clusters, yet the combined effect is pretty pale, since only a few bloom simultaneously and they wither before they are a day old.

Cultivating vanilla

Vanilla is native to Central America, the West Indies and the northernmost parts of South America. It dislikes windy weather, but considers itself well enough watered with around 3 metres (yards) of rain per year. In those lands, it flourishes at every altitude from the sea up to 750 metres (2,500 feet). Cultivated vanilla is sterile, so the plant must be spread by cuttings, which are usually made rather long in order to reach up to a low branch on the supporting tree. They take 10-12 weeks to decide whether to put down roots. As a result, all of the vanilla plants on a farm are really one and the same example. Cultivators can therefore be thankful that vanilla is self-pollinating, and does not need to be fertilized with pollen from "unrelated" plants.

When starting to cultivate vanilla, one must first supply trees for the vines to climb on. Generally, one or two years in advance, fast-growing trees or bushes with sparse foliage and branches just over the ground are planted for this purpose. Once the vines have shot up, they must be pruned so that they do not become too high for the flowers to be worked on easily. After three years, it is normally time for the vanilla to bloom. A healthy mature vine can produce more than a thousand flowers, of which some fifty are chosen for pollination—at most half a dozen in each cluster. The blossoming period lasts a couple of months, with the flowers appearing at dawn.

A complex sex life

We now come to the truly remarkable and difficult thing about vanilla: it cannot take care of its reproduction by itself, but needs to be pollinated by man. Naturally this has not been true at all times and places, since otherwise vanilla would not exist. Yet when people first tried in the early nineteenth century to cultivate vanilla outside Mexico—namely in Java—they obtained fine, luxuriant plants without any seed pods. The reason was discovered only in 1836 by a botanist, Professor Charles Morren of Liège University in Belgium. Vanilla flowers are adapted to pollination by insects and possibly by hummingbirds, so they need human help if these are not available. What it was that originally pollinated vanilla plants, perhaps a species of butterfly or stingless bee, is controversial among botanists. Such ancient benefactors of

Vanilla flowers must be pollinated by hand. This precision work must be done in the morning when the flowers have opened.

A flower for a day

The vanilla flower's stamens surround a fleshy lip which separates them from the "female" stigma. A pollinator takes a special grip on the flower with his left hand, which moves the lip aside and exposes the stigma. Then he lifts the bamboo splinter or a tiny brush in his right hand and picks up the clump of pollen, transfers it to the stigma, dries it off, and fastens it there with his left thumb.

This must be done in the morning, just when the flower has bloomed. A single adept pollinator can get through more than a thousand flowers in one morning. The flowers wither at dusk, and four to nine months must pass before the pods are ready to be harvested. They are picked when about to change colour from green to yellow (fully mature ones are chocolate-brown).

As vanilla is an expensive product, there are reasons to prevent it from being picked and sold illegally. This is done in Madagascar by "tattooing" the pods shortly before the harvest—punching holes in their shells to form, for example, the owner's initials or emblem.

Capturing the aroma

The spice or aroma itself comes from the seed pods, which resemble French string beans. And the longer they are when harvested, the better. A pod length of more than 25 cm (10 in) gives the highest quality. They have no special flavour at the time of picking, for the fragrant aroma develops only during the subsequent processing. This is done by various methods in different places.

In Madagascar, for instance, the fruits are commonly dipped in boiling water for a couple of minutes just after being picked. The result is to stop them from ripening further; but next, enzyme action begins to affect a "glycoside" substance in the fruit, and turn it into vanilla. For this to happen, the pods must have rather well-defined amounts of warmth and moisture. During a couple of

vanilla must, in any case, have vanished even from its homeland, because it is fertilized artificially there as well. And its own pollen is used, which has prevented it from becoming a still more complex plant.

Orchid flowers tend to be very specialized and elaborately structured, with the ability to attract only a particular species or group of insects. Cooperation between the plant and animal is then essential in order for the flowers to function sexually. It was a former slave on the French island of Réunion in the Indian Ocean who, in 1841, stumbled upon a practical way of solving the problem of replacing the long-lost insects as pollinators. Using the sharp tip of a bamboo splinter, he gathered up pollen and transferred it to the well-hidden stigmas of flowers. More or less the same method is still employed, so a lot of work is needed to produce vanilla bean fruits.

months, they are coddled like babies and laid in the sun to cure, then rolled in wool cloths at evening to "sweat" overnight. The procedure continues until they acquire the right dark-brown colour. Finally they are dried and, after about a half year of care, are ready to be distributed. By that time, their surface is often covered with small needle-like crystals of vanilla. Today, notably in Uganda, there are faster methods with fermentation at higher temperatures, but first the fruits must be crushed. A fine aroma is achieved, yet not the classic "sticks" that customers want. Consequently, this kind of vanilla is used mainly for producing extract.

Sticks of vanilla are ultimately graded by quality and size, then sealed in boxes so that the aroma does not evaporate. During production, the fruits' weight decreases significantly, to about a fifth of their weight when picked. The yield of dried vanilla sticks from full-grown, ripe plants can approach 100 kilograms per hectare (or pounds per acre).

Readers may now see why vanilla is the most valuable of all spices except saffron. Countries that grow much of it tend to depend on it economically.

Chemical vanilla

The substance vanillin was first isolated from vanilla sticks in 1858, by a chemist named Gobley. One of his colleagues managed in 1874 to create the substance artificially from glycosides in pine resin. This soon led to mass production—and a depression for natural vanilla. During the 1890s, some even simpler techniques were invented, using clove oil or sugar as the basic material. In time, it was discovered that vanillin could be prepared from (among other things) paper pulp, sassafras oil and wood tar. Moreover, a similar substance was found in tonka beans, though condemned by health officials in the United States as being unsuitable for human consumption. As a whole, these chemical alternatives became a deadly threat to the vanilla cultivators.

Still, there is no alternative when it comes to the recipes that call for a natural vanilla taste, with the extra aromatic substances contained in the genuine product. Personally, I always chuckle with joy when I behold those little black grains in my ice cream, proving that the real thing is at hand.

Soufflé à la vanille

First boil the milk in a 2-litre (2-quart) pot, preferably enamelled, together with a couple of vanilla sticks. Let it stand and cool until it tastes strongly enough of the vanilla, which is then strained off. Set the oven at 200° C. Carefully separate the egg whites and yolks. The soufflé form, which is of cylindrical shape about 12 dl (2.5 pints) in volume and 8-9 cm (3.5 inches) deep, should be smeared with butter using a little paper, even on the upper edge and on the bottom angle towards the wall. Throw on some granulated sugar and roll the form until it covers the inside completely, then shake out excess sugar.

Return some of the milk to the pot and make a smooth batter by beating in the flour, preferably using a balloon whisk. Beat in the rest of the milk, then continue to beat slowly over moderate heat until the batter thickens and begins to cook. Keep beating for half a minute, by which time the batter should have become quite thick. Now remove it from the stove and stir for a couple of minutes more, while it cools until you can touch it. Be sure that the batter does not stick to the bottom.

Up to this point, the recipe can be prepared in advance. In that case, warm the batter carefully to the above temperature before proceeding as follows. Add the egg yolks one at a time while beating the batter. Once all four

INGREDIENTS
(for 4 servings)

two vanilla sticks
1.5 dl (1/3 pint) milk
30 grams (nearly 1 ounce)
of all round wheat flour
5 egg whites
4 egg yolks
a pinch of salt
Butter: 25 grams for the batter,
and 15 grams (soft) for the form
Granulated sugar: nearly 1 dl
(1/5 pint) for the batter,
and a tablespoon for the form
1 teaspoon sieved powdered sugar

yolks are beaten in, add half of the butter. Whatever sticks to the pot sides should be scraped down with a rubber or soft plastic utensil. Strew the rest of the butter over the batter.

Next, beat the five egg whites with a little salt, until they become stiff enough to build small soft puffs when drawn upward with the whisk. Add the sugar and keep beating until that same consistency is reached again. Then immediately stir a fourth of the egg whites into the batter, making it easier to work. Carefully turn down the rest of the egg whites. Best use a rubber or plastic scraper to empty the egg-white dish, then slice down the foamy egg white into the batter, while stirring slowly round in the form. This point is crucial for success—the egg whites must keep their puffiness as much as possible. It should all be ready in a minute, even if some scraps of egg white are left out.

Now put the form in the oven, on a grid about in the middle. Lower the temperature to slightly under 200° C. After 25-30 minutes the soufflé should have risen 5 cm (2 inches) over the form's edge and should be a beautiful brown. It is now creamy inside, but must be served instantly. To become more baked throughout, it must stay five minutes more in the oven. Then remove it, let it stand for five minutes, and strew on the powdered sugar.

How to use vanilla sticks in cooking

Alternative 1: Cut up the stick and scrape its small seeds into the liquid—preferably warm—which is used in your recipe. Then add the stick itself, and leave it for 20 minutes. Taste the liquid to check that enough vanilla has dissolved; otherwise leave the stick even longer. When satisfied, strain off the vanilla.

Alternative 2: Grind up two whole vanilla sticks (about 15 grams, or half an ounce), together with 100 grams (3 ounces) of cube sugar, in a mortar or electric mixer. Let the blend stand in a glass jar with a tight lid for about a week. Then pass the resultant vanilla sugar through a fine sieve. This method yields a stronger vanilla aroma. One can also give sugar a slight vanilla taste by leaving a couple of sticks in a jar of granulated sugar, where they also do not dry out as fast.

Allspice

Pimenta dioica

When the Spanish conquistador Hernan Cortez arrived at Tenochtitlan, the Aztec capital, in November 1519, King Montezuma pretended to be hospitable while actually laying an ambush. Before the conflict broke out between the invading adventurers and the native monarch, they fraternized cordially. Mexican cuisine researchers think it likely that the king once invited his guest to a meal which can be described as "braised chicken in chili and chocolate sauce"—the prototype of the country's national dish, *mole poblano*.

We do not have the recipe from that fateful occasion. But some nuns at the cloister of Santa Rosa, in the town of Puebla, later served the same spicy meal to their Mexican overlord. They also wrote down how they cooked it, and this document has survived.

Not a real pepper

One thing we can be fairly certain of is that the Aztec dish relied heavily on a spice which is familiar today. Internationally, in traders' jargon as well as in German and French, it is called "piment"—and the Latin name of its genus is similar. These terms come from the Spanish word *pimienta* for black pepper. In French, the language of gourmets, "piment" can also mean the fruits of various *Capsicum* species, such as chili, which the Spanish called *pimiento*.

Yet this is misleading: the present spice is neither a pepper nor a *Capsicum* fruit! We may therefore wonder how its terminology arose.

"Allspice"

In the fourteenth and fifteenth centuries, the hunger for spices drove the Spanish and Portuguese to voyage in search of their sources. When Columbus reached the West Indies, however, he found plants that had little in common with those of the East Indies, which he was seeking. Among them were spices unlike the classic kinds that Europe had used since antiquity.

During the next decades, it was realized that the Americas had tasty flora of their own. Some were mild, such as vanilla, while others were pungent and bitter, like the *Capsicum* fruits. In between these extremes fell the above-mentioned spice. Its taste and aroma were so generally pleasant that it soon took the name "allspice" in several languages. Indeed, it resembled not only clove—a close relative—but also cinnamon and nutmeg.

Columbus and other pioneers must have noticed this tree, but they were not looking for it, so they evidently paid no attention. The first interested observer, in 1494, was Columbus' own physician on his second voyage. Still, Alvarez Chanca did not recognize the spice's great possibilities.

Species name:	Pimenta dioica (formerly officinalis)
Family:	Myrtaceae, myrtle plants
Spicy part:	Unripe berries (drupes)
Origin:	West Indies and Central America
Cultivation:	Jamaica, Cuba, Lesser Antilles, Trinidad, Mexico, Honduras
Common names:	French: piment des anglais, toute-épice
	German: Piment,
	Italian: pepe di Giamaica
	Spanish: pimienta gorda
	Swedish: kryddpeppar

PIMENTO. off.
Myrtus Pimenta. Bot.
Nelkenpfeffer.

Appearances matter

When the Spaniards saw unknown spices being used by the native cooks of the New World, it seemed natural to name them after Old World spices. The connection was made either by taste (thus *Capsicum* fruits were called *pimiento*) or by eye: this is how the peppercorn-like West Indian spice came to be named *pimienta*.

These explorers also made the mistake of ignoring others' knowledge of plants. In the 1570s, Francisco Hernandez, a scholar sent out by King Philip II, found the allspice tree in the Mexican province of Tabasco. Soon a colleague stumbled on it in neighbouring Chiapas. As a result, both the *pimienta de Tabasco* and *pimienta de Chiapas* were added to the list of local flora, whereas both of them were identical to the *pimienta de Jamaica* on Caribbean islands!

It was Hernandez who observed that the Aztecs used *pimienta* to spice their chocolate drink. But the fact that only one species was involved—though with variations, as in the size of the "peppercorns" —was not announced until the late 1600s, by the great English naturalist John Ray in his book *Historia Plantarum*. He called the spice "sweet-scented Jamaica pepper", or "allspice". It has names with the latter meaning in further languages, too, such as French and Danish—while the connection with pepper is preferred by still others, like German and Swedish.

Diverse applications

Around 1600, allspice finally began to be exported to Europe. Its popularity grew fast, especially during the next century. By 1800, the British West Indies alone were exporting more than 1,000 tons per year, an impressive figure at that time. The demand has varied since then; but if cooks use allspice less, several industries need it today. Besides perfumes and cosmetics, liqueurs such as Chartreuse and Benedictine contain a good deal of allspice oil.

In the United States, allspice is added mainly to desserts, pies, pickles, fruit preserves, and sauces like ketchup. The Scandinavians strew it on herring that are pickled with vinegar and onions, and in meat stews. Germans stuff it in their sausages. France, on the other hand, consumes little allspice except in marinades and some mincemeats.

A stubborn Caribbean

Allspice comes from a tall tree that grows widely in the tropical Americas—especially in Jamaica, whose allspice is of highest quality and, not surprisingly, enjoys something of a world monopoly. We may remember that the Dutch spice monopoly in the East Indies was broken by smuggling seeds or plants to be cultivated in other parts of the tropics. This has also been tried with allspice, for example in the Moluccas and Ceylon. But success is rare, for the tree flourishes only in its homelands. Elsewhere, it produces either no berries or bad ones. Thus the Jamaican planters have nothing to worry about for the present.

The allspice tree has a slim trunk that sheds its soft, light-grey outer bark every year. It branches high above the ground, bearing pairs of lanceolate leaves which are 10 centimetres long, shiny dark-green on top and lighter below. The leaves contain the same aromatic substances as the berries—primarily eugenol, also found in clove.

Cultivating allspice

The pea-sized berries, holding two kidney-shaped seeds each, become dark red-brown when ripe and dry. But most of their aroma is lost by then, so they are picked in July or August while still green. By the traditional method of harvesting, agile youths climb up the trees and break off the berries, while women and children gather them on the ground to be dried—nowadays in ovens, not sunshine. A tree usually produces 30-40 kilograms of dried berries per year.

A hundred years ago, Jamaica's allspice plantations were threatened by a peculiar fashion. Notably in the United States and England, people began to sport walking-sticks and umbrellas made of allspice shoots. The manufacturers of these items were supplied by cutting down millions of young allspice trees. This profitable but shortsighted way of exploiting one of Jamaica's most valuable resources was at last forbidden in 1882. Otherwise we might not be able to taste allspice today—although the same name has been given to some small American and Far Eastern shrubs with aromatic qualities.

The allspice tree has large leathery leaves and white flowers. It can yield ten times as much spice in a year as does the related clove tree.

Red pepper

Capsicum annuum, Capsicum frutescens

In Budapest during the seventeenth century, there was a pasha named Mehmet who caught sight of a beautiful Hungarian water-girl, and immediately had her placed in his harem. Confined to its exotic garden, she became familiar with all sorts of strange plants—one of them being a vine that bore large, pretty red fruit. These the Turks ground into a powder, which was used to spice food for themselves and the harem ladies. Thinking that she had never tasted anything so good, the girl secretly collected some seeds.

As it happened, she was still in love with a young peasant to whom she had been engaged before the pasha appropriated her. Resorting to her wits, she discovered a secret passage which her master had prepared in case he would need to sneak out or flee from his palace. The girl crept through it every night to meet her lover—and once she gave him a bag of the vine's seeds, telling him to go home and sow them.

He obeyed, and after a year or so, paprika plants were winding round all the gardens and gardeners in the city. The Hungarians went wild about the new spice, especially in the countryside. Shortly afterward, there was a revolution: the Christian armies from Austria expelled the Moslems. In the wake of the nation's liberation, its favourite spice continued to proliferate.

Not exactly a native

This saga about the childhood of paprika is romantic fiction, but it does admit the probable fact that Hungary's famous pepper was brought there by the Turkish occupation. The Greeks had already named black pepper *peperi*, and they used the same word for such "Spanish" pepper when they got to know it during the sixteenth century. Then it was spread to the northern Balkan countries, including Bulgaria, and to the Turks—being renamed *paparka*. Having conquered Hun-

Species name:.........	Capsicum annuum
Family:.................	Solanaceae, nightshade plants
Spicy part:.............	The fruit
Origin:.................	Central and South America
Cultivation:..........	Hungary, Bulgaria, France, Spain, Italy, Israel, USA
Common names:.....	French: paprika German: Paprika Italian: peperone Spanish: pimentón Swedish: paprika

Species name:.........	Capsicum frutescens
Family:.................	Solanaceae, nightshade plants
Spicy part:.............	The fruit
Origin:.................	Central and South America
Cultivation:..........	Mexico, USA (Louisiana), India, Indonesia, China
Common names:.....	French: piment German: Cayenne-pfeffer Italian: pepe di Caienna Spanish: pimiento, chile Swedish: kajennpeppar

gary in 1541, the Turks let some Bulgarian farmers settle there, who had learned to cultivate the new red pepper. And those immigrants are thought to have given the Hungarians their national spice, whose name "paprika" was thus a final metamorphosis of the ancient Indian word for black pepper.

Overlooked by Columbus

But the Hungarian paprika is just one of the many varied forms into which the members of the genus *Capsicum* have developed in different parts of the world, during the five hundred years or so since Columbus discovered them. More precisely, Columbus himself paid no attention to natural resources in the West Indies if they did not happen to be black pepper, cinnamon or nutmeg. The physician he brought across the Atlantic was much more interested. Doctor Alvarez Chanca, from Seville, gave Spain the first description of this new spice, which the natives called *agi* or *aji*, as it is still named today in Peru. A famous Italian author, Petrus Martyr Anglerius, who became a chronicler at the Spanish court in 1487, was able to report in 1493 that the new-found land in the west had revealed a kind of pepper which tasted far stronger than the "Caucasian" type—as he termed Indian pepper, according to an old misunderstanding (see page 105!).

Grown as an ornament

This spicy news made little noise initially, but aristocrats and other people who owned exclusive gardens were excited by the lovely red fruit. They began to cultivate *Capsicum* plants for decoration, just as was done with potatoes when these arrived. After a few decades, however, the fruits' usefulness for cooking was realized, and cultivation started to spread through the Mediterranean.

A result was the migration of one form, paprika, all the way to Hungary. During the late sixteenth century, paprika was also introduced to present-day Czechoslovakia and southern Germany. Yet at such high latitudes, the demand soon died out. It was not until the middle of our own century that paprika enjoyed a breakthrough, as both a vegetable and a spice, into our Western kitchens. Farther east, the *Capsicum* plants had easier going. They were taken by Europeans to places like India, southeast Asia and China — where the most powerful varieties, in particular, have rung the bells in billions of bellies.

A Hungarian plantation, not of paprika, but of its fierce cousin—cayenne pepper.

A taste to match the colour

These peppers belong to the family of nightshade and potato plants, which is full of poisonous herbs such as henbane, thorn-apple and belladonna—but it also includes tomatoes and tobacco. There are about ten *Capsicum* species, and two are extremely important in cuisine. Paprika, or Spanish pepper (*Capsicum annuum*), is the mild and refreshing vegetable, also called "pimiento". Its relatively large fruits, which turn from green to red or yellow, are added to salads and to meat or fish dishes, filled with mince-meat or spiced rice, and laid on sandwiches. An annual plant that grows a metre high, it contains unusual amounts of vitamin C.

This kind of fruit obeys a rule of thumb:

"the stronger the colour, the stronger the taste". Consequently, yellow-white paprika is nicest to the palate. But the thick-skinned yellow variety is more sweet and aromatic, suitable for laying on cheese sandwiches and the like. By contrast, the unripe green type can be bitter and is best avoided. The red paprikas are most tasty, yet they too include mild variants. One is the dark-red "cherry paprika", flat with deep flanges, which comes out rather late in the autumn. The varieties with small fruit have higher concentration of the flavouring substance, and are "hottest".

An explosive powder

Paprika powder is used to make dishes like "goulash". Its source is a variety of plant whose shiny red fruits are comparatively small and conical. As with every *Capsicum* species, the taste comes from a bitter substance called capsaicin, while the colour is due to capsanthin and carotin—the latter being also found in carrots. Capsaicin has such a penetrating taste that one gram of it, added to a basin with ten thousand litres of water, can still be felt clearly! But the taste differs in strength between the mild Spanish and the pungent Hungarian varieties.

Paprika is a spice crop that needs a lot of work, because seedlings have to be grown and then transplanted. Previously, the ripe picked fruits were hung up to be sun-dried for several weeks. Nowadays, of course, the drying is done by industrial methods with warm air. As everyone knows who has cut up a paprika, it contains lighter, longitudinal ridges that carry the seeds. The more seeds and

Paprika powder always looks appealing, but its strength varies according to how many of the seeds and their attachments are still present when it is ground.

ridges are kept during the drying and grinding, the sharper-tasting the product is.

In the finest quality by Hungarian standards, called "delicacy paprika", these ridges have been cut out and only some of the seeds are left—after having been robbed of some of their capsaicin. This mild type is commonest in, for example, the United States. Much sharper is "rose paprika", especially popular in Germany and familiar in Scandinavia too. The Hungarians themselves use a quality somewhere between those extremes.

If you want the spectacle of more paprika colour in a dish, you must obviously choose a mild variety, or else the guests may well lose their heads. And when cooking food with paprika, it is essential not to let the paprika powder be heated too much in oil, which would destroy its excellent colour and taste. So you should brown your steak or chicken, then add the paprika and let it lie while the meat is fried or braised at a lower heat.

Today, paprika is grown as a spice mainly in Yugoslavia, Bulgaria, Spain, Portugal, Morocco, and southern California—besides its classic homeland, Hungary. Before World War II, Hungary and Bulgaria had a virtual monopoly; but the war stopped exports to the West and farming increased there, notably in the USA where paprika had already become fashionable.

Fiery cayenne

The other important species, *Capsicum frutescens*, is used to make such effective spices as cayenne pepper, tabasco and chili—as well as a long list of Indonesian "boemboes", Chinese chili sauces and pastes. This species is

Varieties of red pepper are amazingly diverse. Here is a selection.

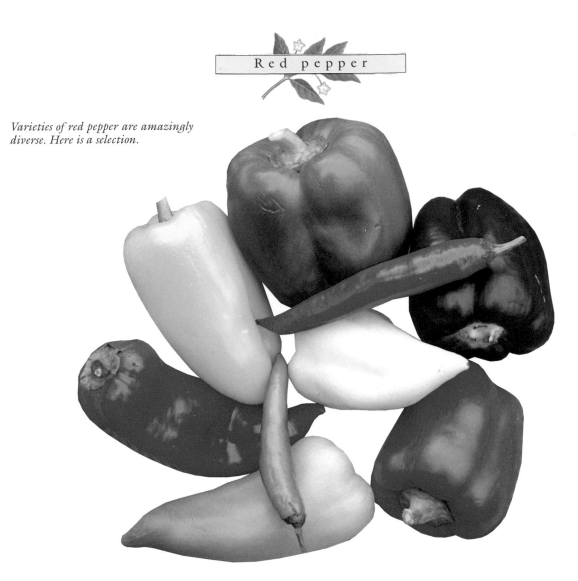

perennial and has a woody stem, growing as tall as a metre and a half. Its fruits are only 2-4 cm long, and nations that enjoy their burning aroma have cultivated ever stronger varieties of them.

The raw material for ground cayenne pepper, which we handle so carefully in our kitchens, is not grown in Cayenne—the capital of French Guiana—but in several countries around the world. African varieties of it contain so much capsaicin that they irritate the eyes and fingers of cooks. If you should ever eat a capsule of tropical *Capsicum*, mistaking it for a piece of tomato, remember that water does not slake this fire: try a teaspoon of sugar instead! But a cooler form of the spice, called red pepper, is made from a variety with somewhat bigger, milder fruit; it is grown especially in the southern United States and in Turkey.

Chili powder

A relatively mild mixture, chili powder, has become popular in both the East and West. It may contain spices like oregano, cumin and garlic, in addition to the stronger *Capsicum* fruits. Such a mixture, although with native herbs, was used by the Aztecs even before Columbus arrived. Their cuisine was partly inherited by the later Mexicans, whose dishes with chili—in particular a meat dish, *chili con carne*—are now served almost everywhere.

Oddly enough, present-day chili powder was invented not by a Mexican, but by English pioneers in Texas, who introduced both the mixture and its name. When we create the combination of cooking and company known as a "barbecue", we are borrowing an old West Indian term, and the sauces or spice blends that we use are originally from Central America. What they all share are, in varying proportions, the two main *Capsicum* species that are discussed here.

Infinite varieties

Alongside these two, which are cultivated widely, there are several with limited uses. Mainly in western India, southern Central America and nearby parts of South America, we find (despite its Oriental-sounding species name) *Capsicum chinense*. The "roqueto pepper", *Capsicum pendulum* or *baccatum*, is most popular in Peru, Ecuador and Bolivia. Distinctively hairy is *Capsicum pubescens*, at home mostly in the Andes and high regions of Central America. Still more confusingly, there are *Capsicum* varieties that look like cherries or tiny tomatoes—but they can be identified at a single bite. One small-fruit type of cayenne pepper, called "bird" or bird-eye chili, has berries that are sun-dried and become very wrinkled.

We may conclude this tour with an old Hungarian proverb: "Some long for riches, and others for fame, but everyone yearns for paprika goulash!" Many of us are better equipped to reach the latter goal than either of the former. And unlike them, it has only delicious consequences.

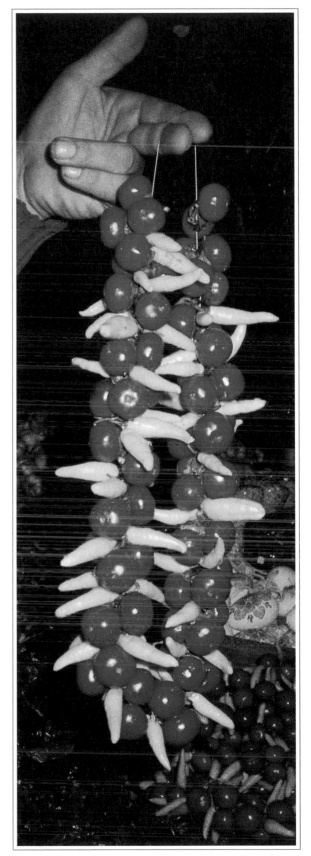

A display of different kinds of red pepper.

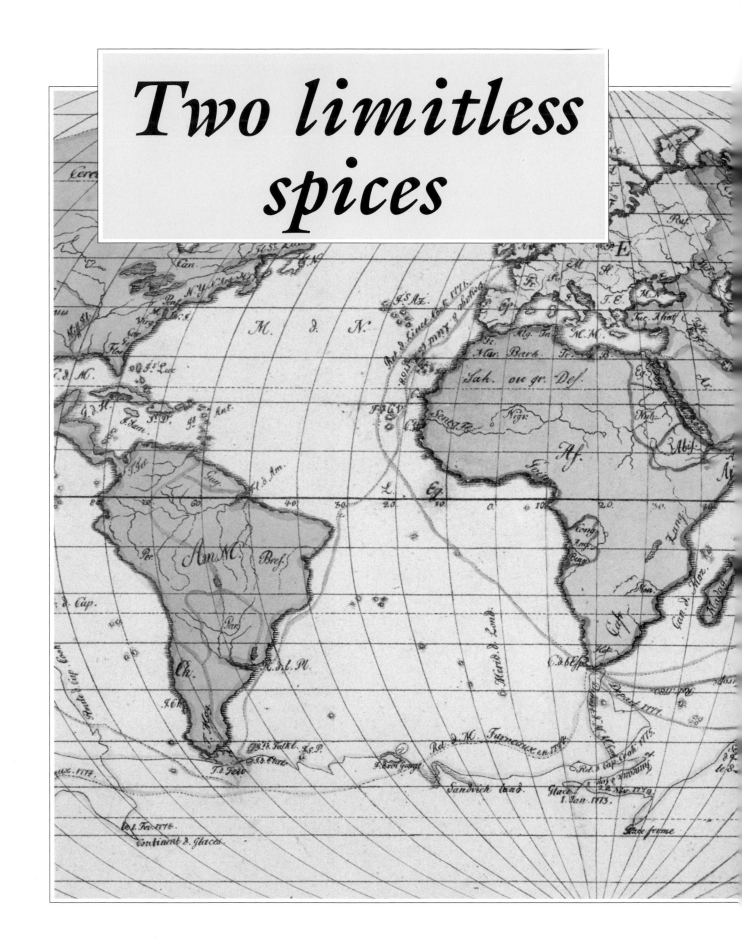

Two limitless spices

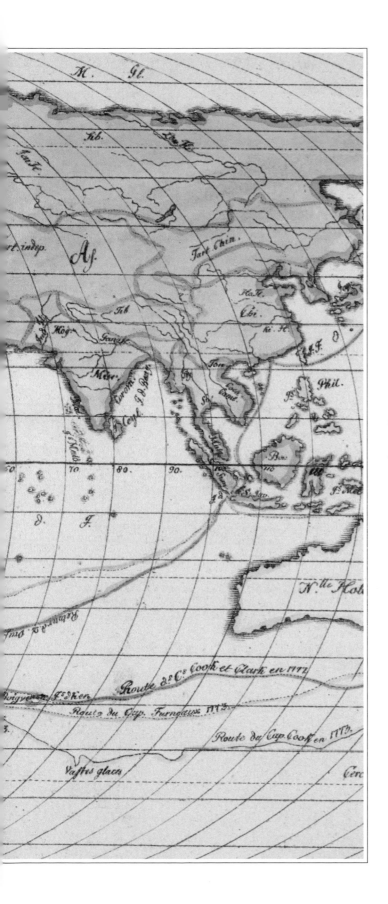

*S*ugar and salt— *tantalizers of taste*

Our sense of taste is admittedly somewhat primitive. The human tongue has only four kinds of taste buds, and they react to only four "basic tastes": sweet and sour, salty and bitter. All of the other sensations we experience as tastes are caused by our sense of smell, which steps in and helps that of taste. It is the combination of those two senses that really enables us to feel, for instance, the aroma of spices. We can hardly forget the flat impact of the finest, best-spiced meal when our noses are plugged by a cold and we have to rely on taste alone.

The same four basic tastes are shared by most animals—even insects. Indeed, we are extremely primitive by comparison with the sensitivity of a butterfly. It can feel the sweetness in a fluid that is 200 times more dilute than the minimum we can taste any sugar in.

Both of the fundamental tastes to be discussed below, those of sugar and salt, can be found in countless foodstuffs; yet mankind has not been satisfied with the latter. Our urge to feel more saltiness and sweetness than nature normally provides has led us to look for rich sources that can satisfy us. This in itself assures us that sugar and salt are spices—they are substances which make eating more enjoyable. And such enjoyment is essential to what we mean by culture.

Sugar

Saccharum officinarum, Beta vulgaris

Among all of the palate's subtle desires, it may have been the craving for sweetness that mankind first learned to satisfy—and perhaps long before the human species was completely evolved. Some apes, in fact, are able to locate the sweet parts of plants that can put a gilt edge on their menus.

Honey—the oldest sweetener

But turning to the aspects of cultural history which are documented in words and pictures, we find almost everywhere in the world that the flower-nectar collected by bees was what originally enabled people to sweeten much food and drink. For ages, they were content to gather honey from wild bees. Old Stone Age cave art in Spain, and New Stone Age rock paintings in India, show how this was done.

Wild bees were such an important resource that they figured in many of the earliest legal codes. A hard problem, solved in various ways by each culture, was how the proceeds from a nest or swarm of bees should be divided up between the landowner and the discoverer. But it became irrelevant when people began to build hives for bees in their own gardens. Nevertheless, for a long time the hives continued to need periodic "refilling" with wild bees, since the bees were smoked to death in late summer before removing the honey and wax.

Beeswax itself was a valuable trade item during the Middle Ages. One of its main uses was to make candles, which were burned by the million in churches. This tradition, strongest in Eastern Europe, was spread by the Hanseatic League of merchants (and still exists today). When the Turks conquered Constantinople and many other centres of Orthodox Christianity, the beeswax market in countries like Poland suffered a severe depression.

Species name:	Saccharum officinarum, sugarcane
Family:	Gramineae (Poaceae), the grass plants
Spicy part:	Juice from the stalks
Origin:	India
Cultivation:	Argentina, Brazil, Colombia, Cuba, Dominican Republic, Mexico, Egypt, South Africa, India, Pakistan, China, Thailand, Indonesia, Philippines, Australia, USA
Common names:	French: canne à sucre
	German: Zuckerrohr
	Italian: canna da zucchero
	Spanish: caña de azúcar
	Swedish: sockerrör

Species name:	Beta vulgaris (var. altissima), sugar beet
Family:	Chenopodiaceae, the goosefoot plants
Spicy part:	The taproot
Origin:	Europe
Cultivation:	France, Italy, Spain, Poland, Great Britain, Germany, Turkey, China, USA
Common names:	French: betterave sucrière
	German: Zuckerrübe
	Italian: barbabietola da zucchero
	Spanish: remolacha
	Swedish: sockerbeta

Beta vulgaris. L.   Saccharum off. Saccharum officinale. Bot. Das Zuckerrohr

A sign of wealth

In prehistoric societies, beekeeping was as popular as the lavish use of honey for sweetening, medicine, and other purposes. Bees were religious symbols of fertility during the Bronze Age, for example in the East Mediterranean area, while honey became a frequent emblem of national riches and individual prosperity. Thus it was mentioned by the Bible, Homer, and the epic poetry of lands such as Finland (*Kalevala* and *Kanteletar*) and Estonia (*Kalevipoeg*)—whose authors sometimes literally rolled in honey.

Even in boring bureaucratic records, the thirst for honey can be detected. Why else did William the Conqueror make sure that the English *Domesday Book* carefully listed the numbers of beehives in every county? Yet the "sweet tooth" of Western Europe was more than its own bees could feed. Honey flowed from Russia, Poland and Lithuania—through the ports of Danzig, Stettin and Lübeck—to Holland and England among other places.

Divine mead

It had doubtless been realized, far back in the worldwide mists of antiquity, that great joy was created by fermenting honey-water to make an alcoholic drink—later called mead. This word, in diverse forms, is common to Indo-European languages, indicating that honey-mead is the oldest such drink in societies speaking those languages. Moreover, it is one of the words that connect the early histories of Indo-European and Finno-Ugric speakers. Finns, Hungarians, and Mordvinians use related names for honey or a drink made from it.

The heady effect of mead, like that of other alcoholic drinks, led people to associate it—and honey, in this case—with the gods, as providers of all good things. Mead and honey often appear in myths and rituals around the world. The beverage that brought poetic inspiration to Odin, the Germanic king of the gods, was mead which had also been "spiked" with the blood of Kvaser, a wise man who was murdered for the purpose. According to a poem in the Icelandic *Eddas*, a gluttonous colleague, the god Thor, drank three whole tubs of mead before he got the strength and courage to fight with giants. In Valhall, the drink-bar of gods and heroes, there was a wonderful goat named Heidrun, whose udders yielded enough mead every day to inebriate the lot of them. Dead souls were naturally given honey in the Elysian Fields of ancient Greece, where honey—often in the form of cakes—was an offering to divinities.

Eternity via honey

It was soon found, too, that honey was a good preservative of food, ranging from fruit to meat. Some of the North American Indian tribes exploited this fact. A short step farther was the use of honey for embalming. Greek authors described the Egyptian custom of, so to speak, "candying" corpses as an alternative to the elaborate, expensive procedure of mummification. When a king died abroad, for instance during a war, he might be sent home in a jar of honey for his state funeral. This happened even to Alexander the Great, according to the historian Statios. A less reliable witness said that Saint Peter, when executed in Rome, was laid in a coffin filled with Athenian honey—a famous brand that was thought to be suitable for the key bearer of Heaven.

Eastern innovations

However, in certain cultures, sweetness was supplied by other means. Syrup pressed from dates, called "date-honey", was more com-

A clump of sugarcane. The grass itself can grow four metres tall.

mon than bee-honey among the Assyrians and Babylonians of Mesopotamia. Some kinds of dates contain more than 50% sugar, and the hot places where their palm-trees grew were ideal for producing such sugar. But the best example was India, and the discovery that a sweet sap could be squeezed out of a plant—sugarcane —which would eventually become the world's main source of sugar.

In the provinces of Bengal and Assam, nature has created a gigantic greenhouse with year-round warm air and wet monsoon winds from the Indian Ocean. These cause the highest rainfall on Earth, and many rivers return the water from the mountains to the coasts. The varying altitude has led to very different habitats for a unique wealth of both animals and plants. Besides a number of our strongest spices, this region gave rise to sugarcane, a thirsty grass. There, its sap contained at most about 5% sugar—but it could be improved by breeding and, with modest rainfall, could develop much more sweetness in its bamboo-like fibres. Many wild plants belong to the sugarcane group, but probably none can be considered the ancestor of our species, *Saccharum officinarum*. This exists only in cultivated form, and is likely to descend from several wild species of the past or present.

When European explorers reached the East Indies and the Pacific Ocean, they found sugarcane as far from Bengal as the Tonga Islands and Easter Island. Yet they saw it only on farms, not in the wild. Apparently it had been transplanted by the Malays and Polynesians who expanded through the island world. On the other hand, those visitors noticed that the islanders never produced sugar from the cane, but munched on it like candy—just as children run about with pieces of sugarcane in, for instance, the villages of eastern India. Or else the cane's sap was fermented into an alcoholic drink—as was undoubtedly also once done in India.

From cane to crystals

We still do not know exactly when sugar was first made by boiling the sap. But it is fairly certain that this happened in India. While the country's oldest writings mention only honey

Sugar in very diverse forms: (from left) fruit sugar, powdered beet sugar, candy sugar, unrefined molasses sugar, sugarcane cubes, three kinds of granulated beet and cane sugar, honey, syrup, and beet-sugar cubes.

grew, sugar-juice and syrup were popular medicines, given for ailments ranging from leprosy to gallstones. Presumably about five centuries before Christ, the Indians began to make the syrup still easier to transport: they cooled it in large flat bowls, forming sugar crystals. Called *khanda* (pieces), the source of our own word "candy", these were lifted out and squeezed in cloth bags to remove more syrup, leaving just firm "sugarloaves" that were ready to be traded.

Sugar farming

India's spice herbs—such as cardamom, cinnamon and pepper—long reached the rest of the world only by trade. They could only be produced in their original homelands, until Europeans took them to tropical colonies. But things were different with sugarcane. It was easily cultivated in various parts of the Orient and Mediterranean.

By the fourth century A.D., production of solid sugar was familiar throughout India. Quick to learn, the southern Chinese were widely growing sugarcane in the fifth century, and their manufacture of sugar is recorded from the seventh century. Sugarcane also crossed the Indus River during the fifth century. In the sixth, it was cultivated—though probably for medicinal uses, as a rule—in Persia, around the old royal city of

as a source of sweetness, these were largely religious literature, and honey continued to be used in religious ceremonies even after the Indians adopted cane sugar. They must have manufactured it by the same simple technique that has been employed widely for similar purposes, such as simmering salt. Thus the Egyptians concentrated grape juice, and the native Mexicans obtained a syrup from sweet corn.

The word "sugar" has been traced back to Arabic (*sukkar*) or Sanskrit (*sarkara*), originally meaning a refined cane syrup. The reason for boiling the sap into syrup was to make it less perishable—a necessity if, for instance, it was to become a commercial item. In India, even far from where sugarcane

Gondeshapur, which had good trade relations with India.

A story in *The Thousand and One Nights* told that Chosroes I, a Persian king (531-579), lost his way during a military campaign and, becoming thirsty, asked a pretty farmgirl for a drink. She gave him a goblet of sugar-juice, mixed with snow. Relishing it, he requested more, and as she obeyed, he thought: "These people must earn plenty of money from such a fine juice, so they ought to pay far higher taxes!" But his sticky idea made the girl's sugarcane refuse to yield more sap. Only when the king repented could he drink his fill. His tooth was thereby sweetened forever, and he started the cultivation of sugarcane near his capital city.

Chosroe's time agrees rather closely with the spread of sugarcane farming in Persia. Even so, trade is a more plausible reason for this—and for the fact that sugar then began to be produced locally on a large scale. It was the Persians who invented sugarloaves with the classic cone-shape. They boiled up the syrup in conical clay vessels, which had a hole in the bottom to let uncrystallized syrup run out. The sugar that remained was pressed, forming a cone. If Persian scholars can be believed, their country was also the first to try refining sugar. It was repeatedly boiled, while removing impurities by filtration.

Arab sugarcane

It was now the Arabs' turn to get to know sugar, and their role became decisive for the westward travels of sugar. The first Arabian court, at Damascus, gained full access to sugar when the Caliph Omar conquered Mesopotamia in the mid-seventh century. In 762 the caliphs moved to Baghdad, centre of the main sugar district at that time. The Arabs fell in love with sugar and took it with them all across the gigantic empire they had created, from Persia to the Atlantic. Sugar was grown throughout the Caliphate—and the refining process was modernized, especially in Egypt with its ancient knowledge of chemical techniques. Egyptian sugar won a high reputation, and the method of cleaning sugar with various chemicals spread quickly to Persia, India and China.

The Arabs' taste for sugar was boundless.

There are tales of nobles who ate and drank almost nothing but sugar from morning till night. Confectioners ruled supreme at the tables of caliphs and princes. In 1040 the Sultan of Cairo, to celebrate the end of the Ramadan fast, threw a party that did away with 73 tons of sugar. Little statues, trees and flowers made of sugar decorated the royal rooms. When the caliph al-Muqtadi married in 1087, his companions consumed over 60 tons of sugar at the banquet. He seems to have had a vast candy kitchen and a veritable army of pastry-cooks.

Sugar to Europe

From Egypt, the trail of sugar led west through North Africa to Spain. An event of great significance for its future was the Arab conquest of Sicily during the eighth century. Europe had, of course, encountered sugar much earlier. Classical authors such as Pliny and Seneca told rumours of an amazing Indian plant from which honey could be squeezed. It would take a while before the resultant juice could be put in solid form, and then traded to the West. Exactly what it was that the Greeks called *sakharon*, and the Romans *saccharum*, is controversial. It may have been Indian sugar, conveyed in small amounts by the Arabs who traded spices. But some historians attribute these words mainly to sweet-tasting medicines deriving from India.

An indication that sugar was unknown as a food in the Roman Empire is that the emperor Diocletian's "maximum price list" for

A seventeenth-century atlas depicts a sugarcane harvest being taken to the press.

goods in the early fourth century A.D. did not mention sugar. Nor did the somewhat later lists of imports to Byzantium from Alexandria. The first certain imports of sugar to the West occurred in 627, when the Byzantine emperor Heraclius brought home booty from a Persian campaign—including a lot of sugar. In the following centuries, Byzantium developed more peaceful trade relations with Baghdad, attracting a stream of Arab sugar. Both there and in Italy, however, it was mentioned primarily as a medicine.

Sugar's breakthrough in Europe owed far more to the Crusades. Through them, many Western aristocrats came into contact with the Arabs' sugary cuisine and learned to like this new sweetener. And when the Normans took Sicily in 1072, a sugar-growing country fell into Western hands at last. Once the interest in sugar was aroused, Italian ports—Genoa and Venice—became the chief means of getting it across the Mediterranean and distributing it to the rest of Europe.

Sugar in the New World

Only fifteen years after Columbus landed in the West Indies, the Spaniards planted sugarcane there, starting a sad chapter in the history of sugar. The plantations on large islands needed plenty of workers, but the supply of natives ran out fast: they died like flies, not least in the mines where the colonists hoped to find gold. Then the great slave trade across the Atlantic became the planters' salvation —and Africa's plague.

The first sugar island was Hispaniola, now divided into Haiti and the Dominican Republic. It passed to French rule in the late 1600s, and for much of the next century its sugar production amounted to half of European consumption. France was so pleased that, with the Treaty of Paris in 1763, she chose to give up Canada and half of the present United States rather than relinquish her West Indian sugar islands. Yet only a couple of decades later, her monopoly fell apart!

In 1791, Hispaniolan slaves revolted and massacred almost all of the French settlers, burning down their plantations and factories. Next, the French Revolution and Napoleonic Wars cut off the trade routes to their motherland. England gladly took over the profitable sugar business, basing it in Liverpool. However, it was prevented for years by Napoleon's "continental system" from exporting sugar to most of the European market.

During the late eighteenth century, German chemists discovered that sugar could be extracted from domestic beets, the species *Beta vulgaris*. The lack of West Indian cane sugar led Napoleon to begin making beet sugar. While his fall brought cane sugar to Europe again, the cheaper beet sugar survived and, with time, became popular in many countries. Even so, world sugar prices still have a crucial impact on the economies of sugarcane lands—chiefly Cuba but also, for instance, Mauritius.

Producing sugar

Sugarcane, a grass of the *Saccharum* group, grows in tropical and subtropical climates. Pieces of cane are planted, and soon send up shoots that can grow six metres tall and five centimetres thick. After 12-18 months, the canes are cut and and new shoots emerge immediately, so a harvest can go on for years. In a sugar factory, canes are crushed between rollers, and the pressed plant parts can be leached to yield even more sugar. A ton of cane provides at least 125 kilograms of sugar. Turning it into white grains and cubes is done mostly in the consuming countries.

Salt

In the dawn of time, relates an ancient Nordic myth of creation, the great void Ginnungagap gave birth to a cow named Audhumla. From her udders streamed four rivers of milk, and she began to lick a rock of salt that lay before her. On the first day a head emerged from the rock; on the second, a man-like chest; and on the third, an entire god stepped forth. He was called Bure, and became the grandfather of Odin, who was the old Germanic king of the gods.

This salt-loving cow is among the features of pagan Germanic mythology which had counterparts in the Vedic myths of India's ancient Aryan folk. Her ancestry can thus be traced back to a common Indo-European culture, several thousand years ago. The way in which she created the gods—representatives of culture—demonstrates the early connection of salt with both the divine realm and human society.

Salt and religion

Already more than a thousand years before these myths were recorded in Iceland, the Roman historian Tacitus described the continental Germanic tribes' belief that the gods were most attentive to prayers if delivered in a salt mine, and that natural salt was constantly produced by fusion of two opposite elements—fire and water—through the grace of the All-Father.

Reverence of salt was hardly confined to the prehistoric peoples of northern Europe. The Pueblo Indians in the southwestern United States also recognized divinities of salt as cultural heroes. And to the Babylonians, salt was a special delicacy of the highest deities, whose tables should never be without it. In Madagascar, the word for salt means sacredness as well. The mythological role played by salt, of course, reflects its central status in daily human life, where salt has enjoyed greater importance and longer use than any other spice.

The functions of salt

To be sure, the stuff in our salt-shakers is not a spice in the botanical sense. Besides its mineral origin, it consists of a simple inorganic substance—sodium chloride—unlike most other spices and aromas. Still, nobody can deny that salt is primarily employed as a spice in our food. Westerners are accustomed to the taste of salt with meals, which tend to seem flat and unappetizing without it.

Salt does, at any rate, exist in our bodies: not only in secretions such as tears and perspiration, but also in muscles and body fluids. We need an additional supply of salt, normally 6-8 grams per day, and increasing with temperature or hard work. Formerly, books about housekeeping recommended that slaves should eat more than 20 grams of salt daily, which

Chemical name:.....*Sodium chloride*
Origin:.................*All the world's salt came originally from sea water. There are two main types of salt: unrefined and refined. The first includes rock salt from mines, sea salt extracted by evaporation in salinas, and lake salt. Refined salt is derived from rock salt, and a chemical process turns it into "vacuum salt", which is the purest form of salt.*
Production:...........*Sea salt in Brazil, France, Italy, Spain, Tunisia, Egypt, Turkey, India, China, USA; rock salt in England, Denmark, Poland, Germany, Soviet Union, USA*
Common names:...*French: sel*
German: Salz
Italian: sale, salato, salare
Spanish: sal
Swedish: salt

Salt can take many shapes even if it all comes from the sea. Shown here are unprocessed sea-salt, fine and crude rock salt, and two large salt crystals.

would have been far too much—in economic as well as physiological terms—if they had not been forced to do sweaty tasks. Yet even we ordinary citizens, who sweat only when jogging or sunbathing, consume a lot more than the essential 5 grams per day. This is due not to a need for extra salt, but to our habits of taste and therefore of cooking.

Salt against staleness

In many cultures, salt has been a very convenient food-preservative. Before industrialization, people have always lived mainly on self-sufficient farms, where some basic foods must be preserved because they are not available all year round. Now that we can buy fresh food in stores at any time, the annual cycle of our forefathers has been completely forgotten. Nonetheless, much of what we eat, explaining that it "tastes good", originated as a means of enabling a temporary food resource to last longer—often for at least a year, until it became available again.

Thus, northern Europeans once drank milk only in the summer, since their cows could not produce milk while living in barns during the cold winter. For this reason, they did not drink all the summer milk but made its fat into butter, and its protein into cheese, which were both salted in order to keep better. Farther south, the cows stayed outdoors and were milked continuously, so vegetable oils replaced butter as a principal food fat.

Salt for fish

Fish such as salmon and herring were easiest to catch when, before spawning, they swam upriver or formed coastal schools, respectively. Large catches could then be stored quickly, but would soon have rotted unless preserved in salt—sometimes combined with older methods like acidification and drying. This requirement gave rise to typical North European staple foods such as salted and pickled herring, stockfish and dried cod, fermented Baltic herring and sea trout. Later

the technique of smoking fish was added, turning the North Sea's herring into kippers and the Baltic's into buckling. Even in the Middle Ages, these products were greatly exported southward, not least to Catholic countries during their periods of fasting.

Preserving meat

Pigs and geese were two domestic animals whose fat was especially attractive as a food. Grazed through summer and early autumn in the acorn-tree forests, stubble and fallow fields, they reached an optimum plumpness in October or November. Then came the slaughter, before they themselves began to use up their winter reserve of fat. The end result was a heap of food that had to satisfy the demands of family and farm until the next slaughter. And the only feasible way of keeping so much meat was to salt it. Thus salt became a main household article in the lands north of the Pyrenees and Alps.

The salt trade

For a thousand years, the production and trade of salt generated wealth for some people and work for others. It was also a cause of war between rulers, and of competition between merchants. One would not be exaggerating to compare the salt trade's importance, for example during the fifteenth and sixteenth centuries, with the political role of the oil trade in our own century.

Nations depending on salt consumed a good deal of it—according to some estimates, as much as 40 grams per person daily in the sixteenth century and 70 grams in the eighteenth. Their populations would probably have been decimated if such amounts of salt had really been digested. However, a large share of the salt was poured out with the year-old brine, before the meat tins and herring barrels were refilled. A part, too, was used by tanneries or fed to farm animals. Despite this, the salty diet was obviously harmful. It explains why our ancestors drank huge quantities of beer, which was needed to flush their long-suffering kidneys. The common man's thirst went beyond the wildest beer-gulping dreams of young people and restaurant customers today.

Im Salzkammergut, da kann man gut

This verse from "The White Horse Inn" may recall the happy days of Emperor Franz Josef, but it would have been just as suitable at feasts in the same mountain villages during ancient times. Around 2,600 years ago, at Hallstatt in Salzkammergut (now the "lake district" of northern Austria), existed one of Europe's first big industrial sites—a vast salt quarry, at least 3.5 kilometres long. The salt was a leading commercial item already in the Late Bronze Age, enriching mountaineers and traders.

Discoveries of salt in the Alps were a foundation of the Iron Age culture in central Europe. The latter, in turn, became the driving force behind the expansion of Celtic peoples across much of the continent during the centuries just before Christ. Salt, bronze and iron were the essential goods that transformed their trade routes into a network,

Mining rock salt in Germany.

kind—such as Bad Hall and Halle am Saale. But the most impressive salt mine in Europe is that of Wieliczka, just southeast of Krakow in Poland. Here, at a depth of 300 metres, seven storeys of passages with a total length of more than 125 kilometres have been dug out, since production began in the eleventh century.

Salt on the continents can also be found in salty lakes, marshes, steppes and other surface features. Great "salt oases", as in North Africa, were exploited in early times. The Greek historian Herodotus, in the fifth century B.C., wrote about the extensive salt trade along caravan routes through the deserts, which has continued until the present day in some places. On the return journey, merchants brought slaves—an equally important object of ancient commerce.

Salt from the Mediterranean

Yet for certain periods and cultures, the primary sources of salt have been the oceans, which contain 2-3% of salt. If all the salt in the seas were extracted, it could cover every continent with a layer 40 metres thick. In the Mediterranean, a central region in Old World history, the salt content of the eastern waters can rise to over 4%. While the Celtic peoples of pre-Roman times obtained salt mainly from the mines in the Alps and Carpathian Mountains, these went out of use until the Middle Ages, because the Romans preferred sea salt. This was produced most easily in an area like western Italy, where the Adriatic Sea receives much river water.

Another such area was the south coast of Gaul (France). From the shores of the Tyrrhenian Sea, the Romans brought their produce along a "salt road", the Via Salaria, to the Italian peninsula and Rome in particular. Even today one can walk out of the city, northward from the Via XX Settembre, and travel the Via Salaria—although not on the ancient paving stones. North of the Po River, a further salt industry was based upon the marshlands around Venice, which earned most of its income from the salt trade before

which only the Roman conquests starting with Julius Caesar would destroy.

There are several theories about why the need for salt grew so great during the Celtic Iron Age. One is that the main diet of animal meat, whose own salt provides enough for humans, was gradually replaced by grain-based food, and especially bread, which requires extra salt. Even nomads and herding folk, drinking large amounts of milk, get their salt quota from the daily diet: cow and buffalo milk can contain up to three times more salt than human milk. Other historians point out that the climate became worse at the end of the Bronze Age, making it necessary in many parts of Europe to keep the livestock indoors in winter, causing the annual cycle of slaughter and consumption which has been mentioned above.

Central Europe is notably rich in salt resources, and not only in the Alps. Saltworks were termed "halls" in Old German, and the map of Germany reveals many names of this it became a famous port for exotic foreign spices. Hence the old verse about the city's dangerous damsels:

"In Venice, why do many whores abound?
The reason, Sir, is easy to be found:
Because, as learned sages all agree,
Fair Venus' birthplace was the salt—the sea."

The Mediterranean salt comes chiefly from Sardinia nowadays, but a good deal is also produced in Sicily, south of Trapani. Turning to the Atlantic, a large salt industry once existed on the Biscay coast of France, and exports from the bay south of the Loire estuary must have reached as far as Scandinavia during Viking times. France's centre of salt extraction now lies on the Peccals coast at Algues-Mortes, an old fortified Crusader port on the Bay of Lions, southwest of Nimes. How big its salt industry was, already in the fifteenth century, is shown by an episode from the city's history. In 1418, it repulsed an attack by the Burgundians, who fell in such numbers that they could not be buried quickly, as sanitation required. So one of the towers in the city wall was filled with salt, and the bodies were preserved there like herring, until a proper Christian funeral was possible.

In warm countries, such as those around the Mediterranean, sea salt is gathered from open pools or ponds, after the water has entered and evaporated. Some areas, as in Greece, have rocky coasts where the waves fill natural hollows, leaving treasure-troves of salt for local use. But on an industrial scale, water is channeled into walled "salinas". A group of them makes a picturesque sight, because they change colour—from pink to light turquoise—as their concentration of salt increases. Tourists in the Canary Islands, unless tired out by the beaches and nightclubs, can still watch how this age-old salt production occurs.

(Left) Salinas in Brittany. Such tanks need careful management to produce high-quality salt.
(Right) A day's yield being collected, and (below) a salina in southern Madagascar.

Salt in northern Europe

However, letting the sun and wind provide salt is a practical method only in regions with relatively hot weather and salty water. In the coastal countries of northern Europe, sea salt must be obtained by replacing the sun's heat above the water with a fire's heat under it—that is, by simmering it. Sun-dried salt has been produced in England only on the south coast during hot, dry years. Salinas were employed on the Danish island of Laesö in the Kattegat, but had to be followed by simmering the water in cauldrons.

The latter procedure was used by the Norwegians to extract salt from the Atlantic. They exported considerable amounts of salt, for example to Sweden, and Oslo was an early salt-trading centre. Olaus Magnus, a Swedish bishop, wrote in his famous *History of the Northern Peoples* (1555) that the Norwegians also tried to bring up saltier water from greater depths, with pipes made from hollowed-out tree trunks. The same approach continued in the eighteenth century on the west coast of Sweden.

Another technique was to burn seaweed, which is saltier than sea water. But this results in "black salt", mostly consisting of ashes and other impurities, such as different types of salts. A variety of "black salt" was produced on the Dutch coast of Friesland, and at Vadehavet in southern Denmark, by burning and boiling the local peat, which is even saltier than seaweed.

Salt routes

The medieval Finns obtained much of their salt by simmering water from the Arctic Sea near present-day Murmansk. It was largely used to salt the plentiful salmon which were caught in the local rivers. According to an account in 1555, caravans of farmers carried salt from there to both Finland and Russia.

Salt production was hardest in Sweden, where pathetic attempts were made to simmer the brackish waters of the Baltic. Sweden longed for a colony in the West Indies, where salinas could be built. Towards the end of the eighteenth century, she finally acquired the rocky little isle of Saint Barthélemy. Yet it

proved quite unable to produce enough salt for the motherland, and its slaves even had to be fed with salted herring from Sweden.

As a rule, the Scandinavian countries found it natural—though not cheap—to import salt from the south. The Hanseatic League of German merchants benefitted by such trade for hundreds of years. Friesland supplied most of the salt for the enormous herring market in southern Sweden during the tenth and eleventh centuries. From the twelfth onward, Lüneburg and other north German sources predominated. Their salt travelled from the mines to the harbour of Lübeck along a route known as "Die Salzstrasse", and the small towns that became rich on this trade are a tourist attraction today. The salt was even sent to Russia, especially via Reval (Tallinn in Estonia).

Simmering up salt was a fairly profitable occupation, although it cost the northern forests a lot of wood. The Scandinavians regarded it as a suitable job for weaklings. Thus the old Icelandic hero of *Frithiof's Saga* (1825), a popular poem by the great Swedish author Esaias Tegnér, presented himself as follows:

"I am now advanced in years,
    and simmer salt on the shore!"

Salt and the State

Governments have commonly improved their finances by putting a tax on salt, necessary as it is to their subjects. The Caesars of Rome were among the first to do so when the coffers sounded empty. Perhaps the most famous salt tax was the gabelle, introduced by the kings of France in 1340. During the sixteenth century it was left in the hands of collectors called gabelleurs, who took all they could get. The task was dangerous, for not only were these men sometimes—and quite properly—murdered, but the communities responsible were frequently punished with plunder by the royal troops.

The gabelle was ultimately important as one of the social injustices that led to the French Revolution. Abolished in 1790, it was revived by Napoleon and did not really disappear until after World War II. Some form of salt tax, even if less severe, has existed in most other countries. Exceptions—so far—are the United States and Sweden.

A monopoly on salt, enabling governments to fix offensive prices, has repeatedly been of political value. The idea occurred already to a Chinese emperor, Huan Chung, in the seventh century. Hungary had a salt monopoly which, in 1597, caused several bureaucrats to be thrown from a window, and also won religious freedom for Protestants.

In our time, salt monopolies have forbidden ordinary people to gather or distribute the abundant sea salt along their own shores. The British passed such a law in India. In 1930, Gandhi and some of his followers protested by marching 300 kilometres from Ahmadabad to a huge salt plain on the coast. He picked up a little salt and travelled about with it for half a year; thousands of poor Indians did likewise, and were arrested. Finally the British realized that their policy was pointless. The salt tax was repealed, though only in 1946, and became a step towards the country's independence.

Salt as a symbol

The Bible's Sermon on the Mount contains a curious expression: "If the salt has lost its savour, wherewith shall it be salted?" This had both a symbolical meaning and a practical origin. The Israelites got their salt from

*A market in Morocco. The great economic importance
of salt throughout the world is reflected in its symbolic
meanings. Primarily it has stood for friendship and
hospitality.*

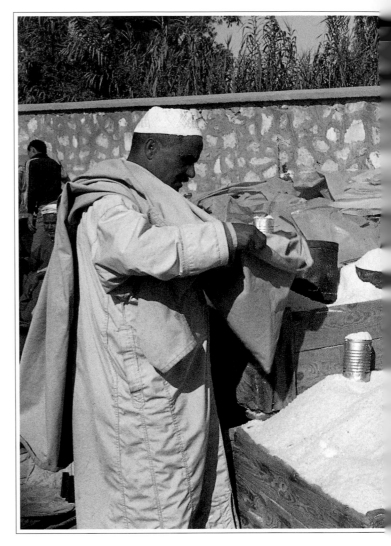

near the Dead Sea, where it was largely
mixed with sand. Rather than strewing the
mixture on food, they put it in a cloth bag
which was placed in the cooking-pot. Soon
the salt dissolved into the soup, leaving the
sand in the bag. Obviously the sand could
only be "cast out and trodden under foot",
as the Sermon continues!

In many lands, salt and bread form a symbol of friendship and hospitality. According
to a tale in *The Thousand and One Nights*, a
thief broke into the sultan's treasure-room
and took a sack of jewels. But in the darkness
he happened to lick a salty stone. So he left
the jewels alone: "One cannot steal from
those whose salt one has tasted."

Germany illustrates another venerable

custom—welcoming new neighbours with a gift of salt and bread. This has even been done recently in Finland. When the Soviet Army left Afghanistan in 1989, compatriots were waiting across the border to offer bread and salt.

Salty remedies

Salt has widespread uses in traditional folk medicine. It was often believed to drive out evil spirits, such as the demons that cause diseases. More surprisingly, an English doctor named William Lee published a book in 1835 about brandy and salt. He recommended that salt be mixed in Armagnac brandy, and every single day begun—by adults and children alike—with a spoonful of this awful potion. It would, he claimed, get rid of rheumatism and scurvy, chilblains and deafness, cancer and scabies and strokes. If drunk by pregnant women, it guaranteed an easy delivery and a healthy child...

The commonest spice families

A symbolic herbal bouquet with two fruit formations

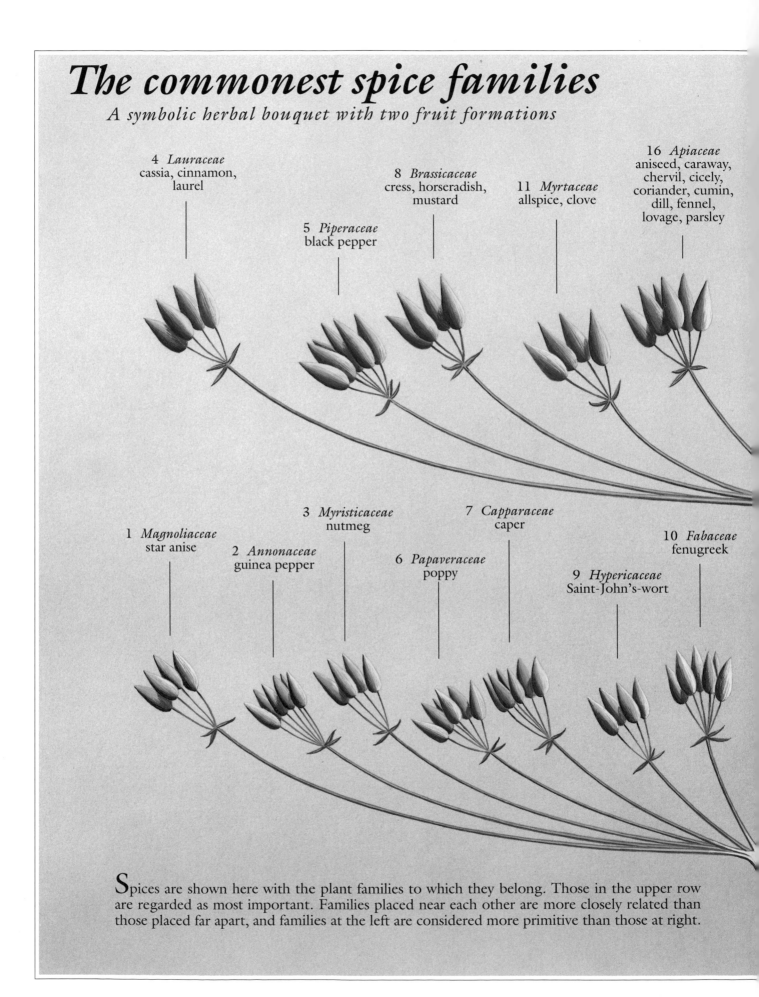

4 *Lauraceae*
cassia, cinnamon,
laurel

5 *Piperaceae*
black pepper

8 *Brassicaceae*
cress, horseradish,
mustard

11 *Myrtaceae*
allspice, clove

16 *Apiaceae*
aniseed, caraway,
chervil, cicely,
coriander, cumin,
dill, fennel,
lovage, parsley

1 *Magnoliaceae*
star anise

2 *Annonaceae*
guinea pepper

3 *Myristicaceae*
nutmeg

6 *Papaveraceae*
poppy

7 *Capparaceae*
caper

9 *Hypericaceae*
Saint-John's-wort

10 *Fabaceae*
fenugreek

Spices are shown here with the plant families to which they belong. Those in the upper row are regarded as most important. Families placed near each other are more closely related than those placed far apart, and families at the left are considered more primitive than those at right.

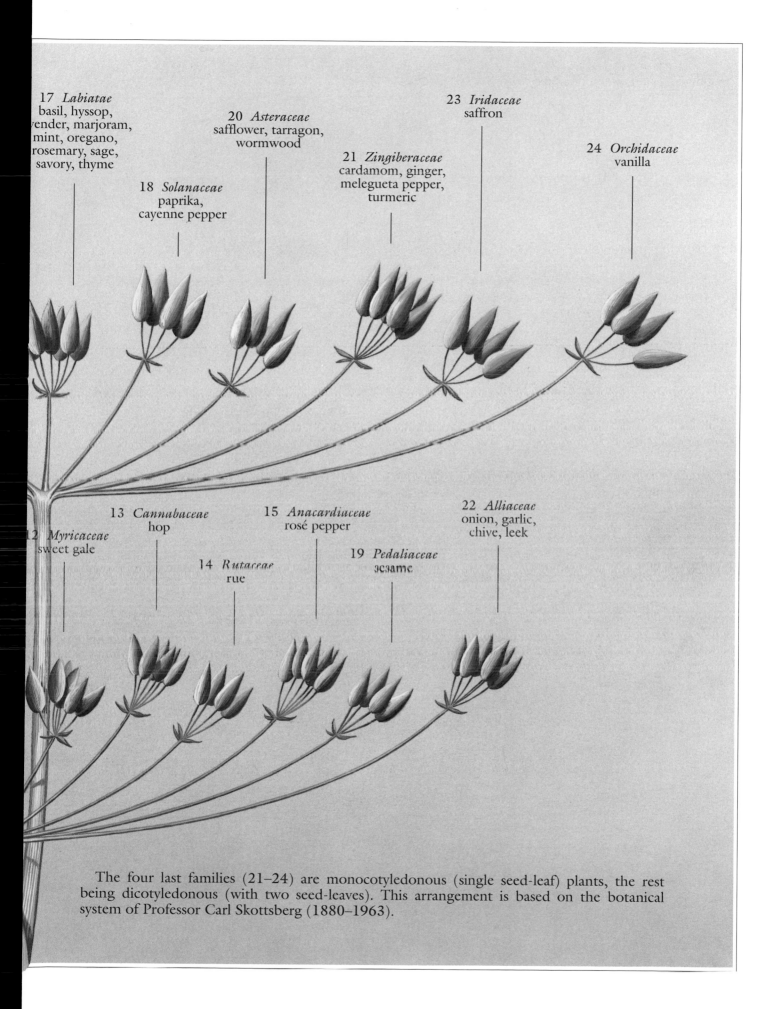

17 *Labiatae*
basil, hyssop,
lavender, marjoram,
mint, oregano,
rosemary, sage,
savory, thyme

18 *Solanaceae*
paprika,
cayenne pepper

20 *Asteraceae*
safflower, tarragon,
wormwood

21 *Zingiberaceae*
cardamom, ginger,
melegueta pepper,
turmeric

23 *Iridaceae*
saffron

24 *Orchidaceae*
vanilla

12 *Myricaceae*
sweet gale

13 *Cannabaceae*
hop

14 *Rutaceae*
rue

15 *Anacardiaceae*
rosé pepper

19 *Pedaliaceae*
sesame

22 *Alliaceae*
onion, garlic,
chive, leek

The four last families (21–24) are monocotyledonous (single seed-leaf) plants, the rest being dicotyledonous (with two seed-leaves). This arrangement is based on the botanical system of Professor Carl Skottsberg (1880–1963).

Illustration sources

Cappelen Förlag AS, Oslo: Page 184

Hjalmar Dahm: Pages 196–197

Rolf Erixson: Page 70

ET Archive, London: Pages 10–11, 16, 42, 90–91, 136, 160, 161

Håkan Forshult: Pages 68, 143

Botanical Library, Gothenburg University: Pages 22, 31, 35, 37, 39–41, 45, 51, 55, 59, 63, 70, 77, 83, 85, 87, 93, 96, 99, 101, 111, 117, 123, 133, 149, 153, 155, 157, 163, 171, 172, 175, 183, endpaper

Gothenburg Museums: Pages 34, 108–109 (photo: Håkan Berg), 112–113 (photo: Håkan Berg), 135, 139

Photographie Giraudon, Paris: Page 126

Edgar Hahnewald: Pages 40, 49, 50, 57, 61, 73, 109, 114, 115, 148, 168, 182, 185

AB Hansson & Möhring, Halmstad: Pages 194–195

Torkel & Elisabeth Hagström: Pages 50, 52, 78

Kari Jantzen: Pages 24–26, 29, 30, 33, 36, 40, 43, 44, 54, 58, 60, 62, 74, 76, 80, 82, 84, 86, 92, 100, 102–103, 106, 110, 116, 120, 122, 125, 131, 132, 134, 140, 144, 146, 148, 150, 152, 154, 156, 162, 170, 174, 177, 186–187, 190–193

Koninklijk Instituut van de Tropen, Amsterdam: Pages 104, 113

Royal Military Record Office, Stockholm: Pages 11, 12, 17, 19–21, 88–89, 124, 158–159, 180–181, 188–189

Mansell Collection, London: Pages 66, 105

Mediterranean Museum, Stockholm: Pages 13, 48

Museo Archeologico, Como: Page 164

Magnus Neuendorff: Pages 94–95

AB Nordfalks: Pages 18, 60, 61 (photo: Raimo Oravia), 64 and 67 (photos: Safinter, Barcelona), 71 and 73 (photos: Raimo Oravia), 119, 121, 134, 137, 138, 142, 143, 165–167, 173 (photo: Ministry of Agriculture, Jamaica), 176, 179 and 200–201 (photos: Raimo Oravia)

Nordic Museum, Stockholm: Page 19

Ingvar Nordin: Pages 39, 51, 53, 57, 72, 78, 178

Torgny Nordin: Pages 12, 114–115, 118

Carin Ohlson: Page 92

AB Pripps Bryggerier, Gothenburg: Page 32

Nils Sandberg: Pages 47, 75, 79, 81, 145, 147, 151

Stiftelsen Skansen, Stockholm: Page 23

Service Photographique de la Réunion des Musées Nationaux, Paris: Page 38

Svalöf AB, Svalöv: Page 27

Ulf Söderqvist: Pages 28, 35, 56, 79 (spearmint), 97, 164, 175 left, 202–203

Charlotte von Scheele/Gothenburg Botanical Garden: Page 25

Museum of Far Eastern Antiquities, Stockholm: Page 141

Subject Index

Species Index